THE MYSTIC ECONOMIST

Clive Hamilton

That which is uttered from the heart alone
Will win the hearts of others to your own.

Goethe

Willow Park Press
PO Box 496,
Fyshwick, ACT 2609
AUSTRALIA

Printed on recycled paper. Typeset in 9pt Bookman Light
Printed by Union Offset Co. Pty Ltd, Fyshwick, ACT

Hamilton, Clive Charles, 1953–
The Mystic Economist
Includes index
ISBN 0 646 16955 6
1. Economics. 2. Environmental philosophy

Cover design by Marje Prior Pty Ltd

The cover graphic is adapted from an alchemical text by Michael Maier (1687),
reproduced by Carl Jung in *Psychology and Alchemy*. Maier's picture is entitled
"Sol et eius umbra", the sun and its shadow. Thanks are due to NASA for
permission to use the photograph of the Earth.

CONTENTS

PREFACE

The arguments of this book run counter to the underlying principles of academic discourse, principles in which we have been schooled from an early age. The academic mode of discourse demands exclusively rational contemplation from which all 'subjective' influences have been expunged. The economics profession insists on this principle of objectivity more vociferously than others, perhaps because it is least tenable there. A book on economics that has its foundations in the knowledge of the heart may appear to be a curious aberration in these days of oppressive economic rationalism, but it is precisely the point of the work to assert the dire need for us to go beyond the obsessive rationality of economics. Economics characterises humans in such a partial and distorted way that most people feel profoundly uneasy about the influence of economics on the world. The environment movement in particular knows that the economic way of seeing things poses a severe danger to the future of the planet.

The ideas that led to this book were first presented to an evening class at the Centre for Continuing Education at the Australian National University in 1990. The students of that class were wonderfully responsive and helped me to develop and refine the arguments considerably. Several people have since provided invaluable comments on parts or all of the book. They include Dr Franzi Poldi, Kathleen Mackie, Father Frank Devoy and my good friends Barbara Lepani, Onko Kingma and Ron Allen. I would like to extend my warm thanks to all of them. Special thanks are owed to Ron Allen for his support for the publication of the book. Marje Prior has kindly contributed the cover graphics. This book is dedicated to my *soror mystica*, Kate Hamilton, whose unfailing encouragement has meant so much.

Canberra

1 INTRODUCTION

We often see economists on television pontificating about the state of the economy. They might reel out a series of predictions about what will happen if the government does or does not undertake some action. For instance, we might hear an economist say that if the government does not lower interest rates then foreign money will continue to pour into the country driving up the exchange rate. As a result exports will be less competitive, worsening the trade balance. This will cause a loss of confidence which will force the exchange rate down, bringing about a harsh and damaging result in the longer run. Usually by this stage, the listener is hopelessly lost because it is not at all obvious why any of these predictions should follow. So we just assume that the economist must know best.

But there is a professional secret behind this pontificating: the economist in fact has almost no idea at all what will happen to the economy and is basing this string of assertions on some theories about economic relationships none of which has been proved or even established beyond reasonable doubt. What the economist is really saying is that if event A occurs then in some circumstances it is probable that event B will occur and if B occurs then it is possible that C will occur. Many other things will happen in the meantime but it is impossible to know what these are.

Some sceptical people have kept records of economists' predictions and tested them against actual outcomes. These studies have shown repeatedly that economists' forecasts are consistently wrong. They are not always wrong because if they were we would be able to predict accurately what will happen, viz. the opposite to that which the economists predict will happen.

It must be asked why modern economics has failed so miserably to understand how economies really work despite 80 years of enormous intellectual effort devoted to the question. This book suggests an answer that goes beyond the usual excuse that our knowledge is still imperfect and more research is needed. The answer is that economics is built on a model of human behaviour in which humans are narrowly depicted as rational economic agents whose purpose in life is to maximise welfare by unrelenting economic calculation. The welfare maximiser, known in economics as *homo economicus* or rational economic man, in no way approximates the complex and subtle reality of human beings and their behaviour, yet economics is constructed entirely on the assumption that *homo economicus* truly represents the essential character of humanity.

Economics has not conjured the notion of *homo economicus* out of thin air, for it does indeed express an aspect of ourselves and a part of the way Western societies function. Advanced industrial society creates in all of us an 'economist within', but we as humans are much more than that. One of the central arguments of this book is that we are social beings as well as private economic agents, citizens as well as consumers, and that by denying us our social and ethical natures modern economics constructs a dangerous and self-destructive world.

As the argument of the book progresses we will explore a more profound proposition: we will ask whether we are not only social beings but divine beings. A thesaurus might associate the word 'divine' with the following ideas: sacred, sublime, godly, celestial, holy, marvelous and spiritual. If modern economics has difficulty accepting the implications of humans as social beings, the notion of the divinity of humans can only be anathema. Indeed, by acting unceasingly to give validity to and reinforce the economist within, modern economics actively denies and suppresses our divine selves.

Many commercial and political forces in society seek to convince us that the path to happiness lies in material acquisition and self-centred pursuits. Economics lies at the very core of these forces and goes further in maintaining that human nature is *essentially* selfish and acquisitive. But for centuries sages and saints from all religious traditions have affirmed that the disjunction between what we consciously believe ourselves to be and what we truly are is the root cause of human misery and that the purpose of life is to find our true selves. Later chapters explore what the truth of this age-old wisdom would mean for the economic ideology of Western civilization.

It will become apparent to the reader that the essays in this book increasingly focus on a common theme, that of the effects of duality. Duality is a word used in Eastern mystical traditions to describe a mode of personal consciousness or awareness which begins from the radical separation of the active subject from the object of awareness. It is argued here that the European Enlightenment and the scientific-industrial revolution of the 17th and 18th centuries have instilled in us such a powerful sense of duality—the separation of ourselves as individuals from the world outside of us—that it has not only reshaped the world around us but has actually provided the definition of what we are as beings.

The idea of the 'economic agent', the concept in modern economics of what we are as beings, is explained in Chapter 2. There the argument is advanced that modern economics is the quintessential expression of the dualistic view of the world and that as long as we hold on to it we cannot attain our potential as humans. In recent times, the environmental movement has caused many people to begin questioning their dualistic perceptions. Chapter 3 examines the attempts by economics to incorporate environmental problems into the economic framework. That essay argues that there are serious dangers in this new economic agenda.

The fourth chapter provides an illustration of the vast gulf that separates the Western dualistic view of the world and a more organic view of the natural world and our place in it, that of the Jawoyn Aborigines. It does this by exploring the remarkable dispute over gold mining at Coronation Hill in Kakadu National Park in Northern Australia, a dispute that saw two entirely different worldviews—one in the pursuit of gold, the other trying to protect a sacred landmark—locked in conflict. The following chapter takes the theme further through a study of our attitudes to money and work and argues that for all of the hard-nosed rational calculation that is supposed to surround these 'economic' categories, they remain at the deepest level sacred manifestations of our attempts to attain divinity.

The sixth chapter elaborates on a way of being in the world that is wholly contrary to our society's obsession with rationality. The symbolic worldview goes beyond exclusive rationality to encompass different forms of knowledge, and we explore the way in which Western society causes us to devalue forms of knowledge other than that arising from rational scientific analysis. These ideas are applied more specifically to environmentalism in Chapter 7 which argues that environmentalism is at its core a reassertion of our mystical relationship with the Earth and that embracing the mystical self is an essential step in our attempts to save the Earth. Finally, Chapter 8 draws together the argument and presents what amounts to a call to arms. The arms that are to be taken up are those suited as much to a struggle within ourselves as against the injustices of the world beyond.

THE ECONOMIC WORLDVIEW

The economics profession has achieved a high degree of influence since the 1960s. We find economists occupying positions of power in public and private organisations that were previously occupied by people with training in law or engineering or the humanities. In the 1970s economics became the fulcrum of political life. Today, in a way that has never before held true, the Treasuries rule the world, and the models of the economists rule the Treasuries.

The ascendancy of economists has been watched by many people with an ill-defined uneasiness. There is a pervasive feeling that economics adopts and applies a distorted view of the world, one that is rigid, partial and doctrinaire, one that lacks compassion, objectifies people and robs us of our humanity. To these people economics seems to symbolise the one-sidedness of the world. The economists have built a giant machine to explain the world and humans must be fitted into the machine so that our behaviour can be expressed in equations.

Economists have become very adept at building complex and sometimes difficult models to analyse aspects of human behaviour. Although economics has employed models since the time of the Physiocrats in the 18th century, today it is *de rigueur* to express economic thought in the form of mathematical equations. The economists construct their models to represent a certain view of the world. The human actor in the economic world must be moulded and shaped so as to conform to the well-defined parameters of the model. While models can undoubtedly be very useful in pointing to some significant forms of relationship between economic variables, it is a fundamental mistake of economics—a mistake which provokes constant hostility from non-economists—to confuse the models with the economies they represent. Carl Jung once said: 'One ought not to go to cadavers to study life'.[1] Economies are living systems. That is not simply to say that they are dynamic—machines are dynamic too—but that they revolve around living humans who often behave in impulsive, chaotic and whimsical ways.

The economics profession actively encourages the objectification of humans to the exclusion of living people. In a recent survey of American graduate students of economics, respondents were asked which of several characteristics are most likely to place students in the fast track of professional success. Ninety-eight percent said that 'excellence in mathematics' is 'very important' or 'moderately important'. Only three per cent considered 'A thorough knowledge of the economy' to be 'very important', while 68 percent thought that it is 'unimportant'.[2] J. K. Galbraith has written that universities today are producing 'a generation of *idiots savants*, brilliant at esoteric mathematics yet innocent of actual economic life'.[3]

An economy is made up of living people and people have a complexity that is beyond the ability of models to capture. But modern economics remains entrapped in the mechanical view of the world that was propagated by nineteenth-century science. The mechanical view is founded on the analytical process, that is, the process in which the object of study is broken down into its constituent parts in order to understand how it works. We will return to this theme. Here we simply observe that the essence of the human cannot be found by analysing our constituent parts, even if these parts are assembled into an extraordinarily complex model, for the essence lies in its wholeness. Goethe expressed it precisely:

> To docket living things past any doubt
> You cancel first the living spirit out:

> The parts lie in the hollow of your hand,
> You only lack the living link you banned.[4]

Neoclassical economics insists on its objectivity, on its status as a product of pure thought. It is therefore in an impossible position when it comes to assessing the arguments of this book because they are to be apprehended and known as much by our feeling natures as by our intellectual powers. For economics, and indeed for academic social science more generally, this is an open invitation to dismiss the arguments as 'emotional' and therefore invalid. But economics deals with humans and humans are emotional creatures; to deny our feeling and spiritual natures is precisely the error of modern economics. To understand something only by the intellect is a very incomplete understanding.

Moreover, modern economics is not the rational, value-free science it pretends to be but is actually driven by a powerful emotional need, the need to be detached from one's feelings. The retreat to the intellect is an emotional response to fear. Morris Berman makes this point strongly in his discussion of academic history. He observes that the Scientific Revolution—of which economics remains a faithful child—saw an intellectual rejection of the sensual, visceral appreciation of the world.

> Yet if the truth be told, it is not that the emotional life got repressed, but that one particular emotion triumphed above all the rest. "Emotionless" activity, eg., scientific and academic detachment, is driven by a very definite emotion, viz. the craving for psychological and emotional security.[5]

Perhaps it is the imposition of this psychic distance between the intellectual and the visceral that makes economics so boring, the 'dismal science' in which sensual life itself is banished. Practitioners of economics tend to display an extreme form of obsessive rationality involving a suppression of their feeling natures and a deep split between their intellectual and emotional selves. Strict rationality and denial of feelings is held up as the most laudable quality of economic analysis, just as it is in the society of adolescent boys struggling to find their manhood. Economists appear to have become stuck in this adolescent phase. This fact helps to explain why the profession is a largely male preserve, for the emotions of modern patriarchy—the need to control, competitiveness, the pursuit of omniscience and obsessive rationality—are those of modern economics.

THE ENVIRONMENTAL REBUKE

The environmental movement has posed the most serious challenge to the economic worldview to date. It has compelled us to reexamine what it is that is valuable to us and indeed what we mean when we say that something is valuable and therefore worth having. Environmentalism has provided this challenge by its insistence that there are alternatives to the ideology of economic exploitation, that the world can be thought of as a living environment as well as a set of natural resources, and that there is something deeper and more human beneath the rational calculator of economics. This has led to a challenge to the very notion of economic value. In economics something in the world is valuable if it gives pleasure to the individual human, and the extent of its value is the extent of the pleasure it gives. The extent of pleasure, relative to other economic goods, is measured by its money price.

We will see in the next chapter that the economic way of thinking begins and ends with the concept of 'relative utility' or relative satisfactions. People are thought to trade off progressively one possible outcome (a bundle of 'goods') against another possible outcome up to the point where they are indifferent between outcomes. This applies to buying a car or deciding complex environmental or resource use issues. Thus if the net utility of the gainers from a property development outweighs the net disutility (dissatisfaction) of the losers then society benefits from the development and it should go ahead.

This approach is known as utilitarianism and is particularly associated with the 19th century British philosopher Jeremy Bentham. The problem is that the utilitarian approach of economics cannot go beyond relative utilities; in particular, there is no place for the ethics of a decision. But environmental decisions are seen by most people as involving vital moral questions. Environmentalism dares to suggest that there are ethical values in addition to economic ones, indeed that there are values that are independent of the human valuer. Here we have a challenge to the very notion of ourselves as rational economic calculators who make decisions by weighing up the benefits and costs of decisions to ourselves. We will see that when faced with critical decisions such as those concerning biodiversity (what we lose when species become extinct) and global warming the policy implications of the two ways of seeing the world are vastly different. The difference between the two ways of seeing the world suggests that to become an environmentalist is for many people as much a personal struggle (against the economist within) as a battle against corporations that pollute the rivers and denude the landscape.

The conservation debate has emphasized the impact of the degradation of the natural environment on our accustomed material living standards. But the above suggests that in addition there is a growing questioning of the ethical principles that underlie our attitudes to the natural environment. Some believe that our current crisis is due fundamentally to a set of beliefs about ourselves and the world that is hostile to the natural environment and therefore, if we could only recognise it, hostile to ourselves.

It is not enough, then, to want to preserve the tropical forests because they are the lungs of the Earth and the source of new medicines. It is not enough to oppose pollution of the sea because it harms the fisheries and the beaches. To make a decision that could result in the extinction of a species is not a question of which path will render greater satisfaction to humans. It is a moral decision. There may be other moral issues that enter the decision, but fundamentally it is a moral decision which no amount of economic calculation can resolve.

This emerging environmental ethic—one that centres on our duty to act as custodians of the Earth's resources—has arisen not out of processes of rational analysis, but out of an understanding of how we feel about ourselves and our relationship to the world. Indeed, after more than two centuries of domination by rationalism, this new ethic is reaffirming the validity of acting according to the imperatives of our feeling nature rather than always succumbing to the arguments of the intellect. This of course is anathema to economics.

The growth of environmentalism in the West comes at a time when increasing numbers of people see their lives as essentially meaningless. Although it is very hard to put a finger on it, many now question the authenticity of their lives—of their work, of their personal relationships, of their relationships to themselves, and of their relationships to the natural world. The great American mythologist Joseph Campbell argues that what we lack and what we seek is the experience of being truly alive, alive in a way that allows our external lives to be an expression of our innermost being, of our true natures as humans.[6]

Somehow the fulfillment that material wealth seemed to promise has eluded us. If money and material acquisition cannot bring fulfillment to life, what can? The extraordinary flowering of the environmental movement in the West is one of the most potent signs of the new mood of doubt and the new desire to change. The strength of environmental concerns among ordinary people appears to be remarkably strong and cannot be explained solely by concern about the economic costs of environmental degradation.

Environmentalism, then, touches on some deep feelings. While there are very good arguments for greater attention to conservation of the natural environment that draw on the threats to our material living standards, there is a deeper strain to the environmental movement, one that denies that the pursuit of the good times is enough in life. This deeper strain expresses the doubts that many people are having about the self-centredness of their existence. It asks people to care about something bigger and more important than themselves and to do so for selfless reasons. It is an expression of a deep and mostly unconscious feeling many have that the collective psyche of the world has become dangerously unbalanced—that there is too much self and not enough other, too many commodities and not enough belief, too much masculine and not enough feminine, too much rationalism and not enough intuition.

BEYOND RATIONALITY

A central theme of this book is Western society's obsession with rationality. Human reason is a wonderful thing; and many argue that our problems are due to an insufficiency of it. But I will argue that obsessive rationality is a product of duality, of separation from the world, and is therefore psychologically crippling. In our attempts to apprehend, understand and control the outside world, we apply rationality to it. But, as Chapter 6 in particular argues, there is a mode of awareness beyond the rational that can reveal knowledge at a level inaccessible to even the most brilliant rational mind. It is a mode of awareness available to all of us.

Environmentalism wants to go beyond obsessive rationality. The natural environment is the warp and weft of the symbolic world within, the world that gives us access to 'the beauteous forms of things', as Wordsworth put it. It is not just the wilderness out there that we want to preserve but the wilderness within, the deep ground of being that has been progressively buried beneath layers of rationality, materialism and alienation since the time of the scientific-industrial revolution.

If there is a central philosophical position that is articulated by the environment movement, it is its opposition to anthropocentrism, the idea that the world revolves around humans, and that natural resources are valuable because they serve our needs. This 'instrumentalist' idea is so fundamental to economics that it is never even raised as an issue. But within the environment movement there is a strong feeling that sentient beings other than humans have value for their own sake. The ethical position of this book does not concur wholly with this biocentric view. The biocentric view of the world leaves many questions unanswered; there is no place for the inner world of humans and its unity with the natural world. To transcend dualism is not to deny ourselves but to conceive of ourselves within the whole.

The question is not whether humans stand at the centre of the Earth, but what sort of humans stand at the centre of the Earth. Native peoples such as Australian Aborigines and Native Americans saw it as being in the natural order of things that they should kill some animals to survive. But it was of profound importance to the well-being of the Earth that they adopted the right attitude in killing them. It was not inconsistent to honour an animal and to kill it. This is in acute contrast to our own attitudes when taking from the natural world.

There is a natural order in the world. Humans are special; our consciousness sets us apart, our ability to be moral or immoral, our ability to think about thinking, to choose to be with god or not. Frogs inescapably express frog nature; storks inescapably express stork nature; but humans can deny human nature. The historical course of our species is not a process of straying from and then being brought ineluctably back to equilibrium, but a question of conscious individual and social choice. There is little doubt that humans are capable of destroying the world beyond the point of no return.

The question we must face is whether we see our position at the top of the natural order as an opportunity to dominate and exploit the natural world or as a moral responsibility to protect and nurture it. Do we act as the dictators of the natural world or as its guardians? We are the only creatures to be presented with this divinely-inspired choice. The scientific-industrial revolution was a critical turning point in the history of our species for that reason. We are offered the choice of seeing ourselves as separate from Nature or as part of it. This is the essential moral question that the environment movement has resurrected.

It is apparent, now that the ecological equilibrium of the planet has been disturbed, that the way humans are answering this question, this truly earth-shattering question, is the most important decision humanity will ever make. It is also clear how this decision is inextricably linked to the way we conceive of ourselves as beings; whether we see ourselves as isolated, rational, self-centred, calculating individuals or as inseparable parts of the Earth with special responsibility for its care. We should humbly accept our earthly responsibility.

Some people accuse the conservation movement of campaigning with quasi-religious fervour. But if religion means a return to the deepest spiritual and moral values, a reconnection between ourselves and our source in the natural world, is that not a cause for celebration? Are not the gravest ills of our society, and the gravest ills of ourselves, due to the selfishness, the greed, the alienation and the ingratitude that grow directly from the separation of our daily lives from our true natures? I am not suggesting that we replace science and economics with religion. I am arguing that we need to be chemists and alchemists, economists and moral philosophers, rational thinkers and numinous believers. In other words, we need to transcend duality and become whole.

1 Foreword to the *I Ching (Book of Changes)*, translated by Richard Wilhelm, Third Edition (Arkana, 1989, p. xxix)
2 David Colander and Arjo Klamer, 'The Making of an Economist', *Economic Perspectives*, Volume 1, Number 2, Fall 1987
3 Quoted in Colander and Klamer, *ibid.*
4 Johann Goethe, *Faust*, Part One (Penguin, London 1949, p. 95)
5 Morris Berman, *Coming to Our Senses: Body and Spirit in the Hidden History of the West* (Bantam Books, New York, 1990, pp. 112–113)
6 Joseph Campbell, *The Power of Myth* (Doubleday, 1988)

2 THE ECONOMIC WAY OF THINKING

Before World War 2 economics was a discipline in which there were several grand competing schools of thought. There were Marshallians, Keynesians, Ricardians, Austrians, Marxists and German Institutionalists, as well as a diverse array of individuals with their own well-developed positions on various aspects of the economy. All that has disappeared. In the 1960s and 1970s economics came to be dominated completely by a single theory, that of neoclassical economics. Generations of students have now been raised on the text book by Samuelson, the standard for many years, and are unaware that there are alternatives to neoclassical economics.

The dominance of neoclassical economics was related to the shift in world economic supremacy from Europe (especially Britain) to the United Sates. In the post-war era the prescriptions of neoclassical economics were consistent with the domestic and global economic policies of the USA. There developed in the discipline of economics an extraordinary conformity of views which saw non-believers marginalised by the profession. There were some well-known purges of university departments. A few non-conformists, like John Kenneth Galbraith, managed to achieve prominence but they were dismissed as populist 'journalists' by the mainstream of the profession. It became no longer necessary to distinguish one brand of economic theory from another because there was only one brand. To talk about economics meant to talk about neoclassical economics.

The total victory of the neoclassical school occurred at a time when economics became far more important in the world of affairs, when governments became wholly preoccupied with economic issues and the economic implications of non-economic issues. This gave mainstream economist tremendous influence over the advice governments were receiving. This advice was based on a single truth that had been established unassailably in the journals and the textbooks. The single truth was that welfare will be maximised when markets are free. This truth was repeated so often as to become an incantation, one that in the Reagan and Thatcher years of the 1980s mounted to a deafening roar. Every piece of policy advice today is underwritten by the assumption that free markets will produce the best outcome. If it is not possible to have free markets then governments should do all they can to simulate the operation of them. Government intervention became the *bête noir* of the economics profession; many economists quite literally have a visceral reaction against it. The economists began to behave like the pigs in Orwell's *Animal Farm* chanting 'Free markets good, intervention bad. Free markets good, intervention bad.'

This book is about the impact on society and on ourselves of modern economics. By 'modern economics' or just 'economics' I mean neoclassical economics. I will not adopt the simplistic argument that economics is something pernicious that is being imposed on us, but that modern economics has in some crucial respects grown out of us, that we carry around an 'economist within', even if we know nothing about economics or reject it vehemently. It will be appropriate then to begin with an exposition of the basic building blocks of modern economics.

THE ECONOMIC AGENT

Modern economics begins with the seminal idea of the economic agent. The economic agent is trenchantly an individual and the economy of modern economics consists of a collection of discrete individuals who interact with each other through well-defined forms of economic behaviour. This economic behaviour consists of a series of choices among goods.

The theory of consumer choice provides the foundation stone of modern economics. It was originally founded on the notion of 'utility', a measure of happiness, and 'utility functions' which purport to show the extent to which happiness increases as the quantity of goods consumed increases. Every good yields a degree of utility that gives happiness. The quality of utility provided by all goods is the same so that different bundles of goods can be compared by adding up the amounts of utility each good bestows. The idea that individual happiness depends on the amount of this single variable that is poured into the consumer is absolutely fundamental to economics[1]. Different types of goods are made commensurable by the fact the people make choices and thus trade-offs between them.

The concept of utility has been plagued by logical difficulties of interpretation and measurement to the point where it has been hounded from the more respectable textbooks. Nowadays, microeconomics texts can expound the theory of consumer choice using only the concepts of 'preference' and 'indifference' without recourse to utility. The safer but less useful device of the 'indifference curve', described below, has replaced the utility function. However, in policy-relevant applied work economists use (sometimes unwittingly) the utility function in order to provide a numerical representation of the ordering of preferences of individuals and to compare the preferences of different agents. Indeed, this is the entire basis of welfare economics and of the set of ideas that underlies all economic debate aimed at influencing the way economies actually work.

Textbooks on microeconomics begin by constructing a model of consumer preferences for the range of goods available. It is assumed that what has gone into the formation of personal preferences, the forces that create preferences, are not relevant. We desire that which we desire. Taking consumer preferences as the starting point of economic analysis also presupposes free will. The whole structure is built upon an idealised relationship in which free and unencumbered consumers confront an array of goods with only the task of calculating the trade-offs standing between themselves and maximum satisfaction.

By beginning with preferences expressed in markets, and accepting that we know what preferences are, it is easy to express the preference relationship pictorially through the device of the indifference curve shown in Figure 1. Figure 1 shows the simplest case of only two goods, x and y. The indifference curve I shows the combinations of quantities of x and y between which the consumer is indifferent. Starting from point A and moving to the left, the curve becomes steeper because as the amount of y falls greater amounts of x are needed to compensate.

The indifference curves show the trade-offs among goods, with each curve representing a different level of total

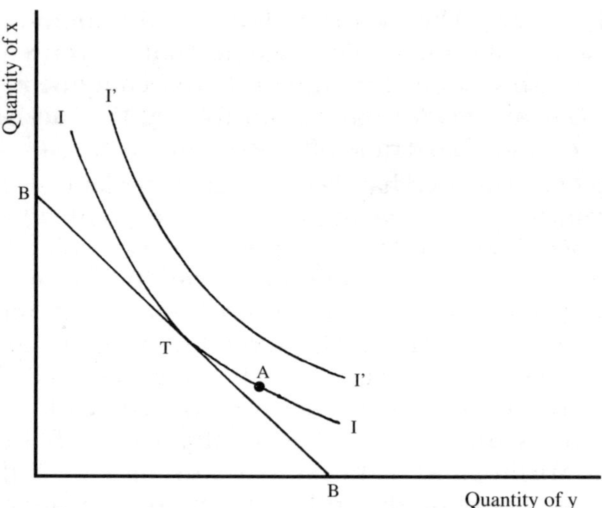

Figure 1 The indifference curve

satisfaction. Thus the line I' shows the range of trade-offs between quantities of x and y which yield equal levels of satisfaction; but this level is higher than that shown by curve I. A budget line shows the trade-offs between x and y that are physically possible given the limits of our income and prices. In the figure, the budget line BB shows the combinations of x and y that are possible with our level of income at the given prices of x and y. We can maximise our 'utility' at the point where the budget line just touches one of the indifference curves. In the diagram this point of tangency is at point T.

While in principle the idea of an indifference curve is enough to construct a microeconomic theory, in practical applications the utility function is needed. The utility function is essential to turn the idea of preference orderings into something that can give measurable conclusions about the way the world actually works. It is usually written in the following form:

$$U = f(x, y, z)$$

so that U, the total amount of utility, depends on consumption of the goods x, y and z, in a world of three goods, say cars, clothes and beer. In other words, our level of happiness U depends on the amounts of x, y and z we consume.

While some of the imperfections of the utility function have been recognised within the discipline of economics for a long time, this has not prevented its extensive use in theoretical and applied work. It is very useful because it provides a numerical representation of preference orderings. The value of each possible consumption bundle can then be ranked. Certain forms of utility functions can actually tell us the extent to which a consumer prefers one good over another, that is, how much more happiness we get from an apple compared to an orange. In the end, these relative satisfactions are always measured by the prices consumers pay for them in free markets.

Maximising welfare, then, is simply a question of dividing one's income between the goods available in accordance with one's preferences. Is this not a simple description of the fundamental act dictated by human nature? There are several serious problems with this approach. The framework assumes first that the essence of welfare is consumption, that more consumption means more happiness, a supposition that we have begun to criticise and will have much more to say about later. Secondly, the situation posited is an artificial one. The economic problem is defined as one that begins with consumers who are faced with a choice between goods put in front of them subject to the constraint provided by a given income. But a great deal has happened to get the consumers there in the first place and their decisions have implications that go well beyond the consumption of the goods chosen to 'maximise' their objective functions. The situation further assumes that the consumer is a separate, isolated individual, a receptacle into which goods are poured to produce 'welfare'. It assumes that the things that are chosen are external to the consumer; there is no place for internal 'economic' needs such as the need for satisfying work or the need for self-expression. And most importantly, there is no place for power, or personal relationships other than market ones, which we all know are crucial to our well-being, even in our strictly 'economic' activities such as shopping and work. In the modelled economic situation, the individual stands entirely alone; no other person exists, there are only commodities.

The economists' felicific calculus associates individual choice with maximisation of happiness. The association extends to trade-offs throughout life and across all situations that involve economic decisions, including choices about the natural environment. This applies to the whole range of human behaviour, from the situation where an individual confronts a good with a price and must decide whether the utility to be derived from personal consumption exceeds the money price, to complex resource development decisions where the utilities and disutilities (negative impacts on welfare) of various groups are aggregated. Take, for example, the trade-off between use of an area of land as a local picnic spot as against its value for sand-mining. For the economist it is simply a matter of establishing the value of the land as a picnic spot, perhaps by asking people how much they would be willing to pay to keep it unspoiled, and comparing this with the value of the mineral sands that would be mined. The ways in which this is done in practice are discussed in the next chapter.

The point to be stressed here is that the economic way of thinking begins and ends with the notion of relative utility. People trade off one possible outcome against another up to the point where they are indifferent between outcomes. This applies to purchasing cars or deciding whether to log a pristine forest. If the net utility of the gainers from an action or a development outweighs the net disutility of the losers then society benefits from the action and it should go ahead. (This is known as a 'potential Pareto improvement'.) The process of comparing costs and benefits to maximise net satisfaction determines whether an action is right or wrong. This philosophy of utilitarianism, associated as we have seen with early nineteenth century British social philosophy, was long ago rejected by social scientists outside of economics because it fails to account for the complexity and contradictions of human behaviour. Economists generally do not recognise it as one of several possible moral philosophies but believe that utilitarianism simply expresses how the world is.

The fundamental problem with the Benthamite utilitarian approach is that it ignores the ethics of decisions; it actually excludes morality from decision making because the calculus of utility itself determines what is right and wrong. An action is right if the increase in utility of the gainers outweighs the decline in utility of the losers. It would be a *non sequitur* for the economist to argue that one of the benefits of taking a particular action is the utility to be had from 'doing the right thing'. To determine what the 'right thing' is, is the purpose of the exercise[2].

Utility functions, then, are the corner-stone of individual economic behaviour. Economics does not consider where these utility functions originate or how people's desires are formed. Desires are taken as a given; sociologists and anthropologists may want to study their origins[3]. Economics is confined to the 'economic' implications of these preferences. Whatever the outcome of the economic process, it is always and everywhere a product of many individuals expressing their preferences. This takes on an almost religious significance in the minds of economists and can be used to justify all manner of social perversion. Even the massive foreign debts of some Third World countries can be dismissed as simply the result of borrowers in those countries expressing their preference for consumption now and saving (to pay off the debt) in the future—a so-called intertemporal consumption choice. The roles of international banks, fluctuating commodity prices, import dependence, lavish consumption by elites and corruption in government are dismissed with the flick of a theoretical wand.

Of course, economics recognises that individuals are, in some respects, social products: their tastes are formed in large measure by social forces, preferences may include preferences for social goods and markets are collective institutions. But at any point in time all of this is history and the individual stands alone, a disconnected mind free to make decisions with the goal of maximising their personal welfare. A vital political ingredient of this is the idea that individuals have free will, that they are free to make choices about their own interests subject to the material constraints of their environment. The political importance of the notion of free will in justifying the products of our economic system cannot be stressed too strongly.

The economists' concept of the individual is a truly fundamental one. It inheres deeply in our own intellectual perceptions of ourselves so that it seems, at first glance, to be an indisputable starting point. The individual appears to be a discrete agent who acts on the world in order to maximise his or her welfare or well-being. Sometimes this is what we see other people doing, and it is perhaps how we interpret our own activities.

The individual or agent in modern economics is known as 'rational economic man' or *homo economicus*. Economic agents are taken to be rational in the instrumentalist sense that they make choices about their purchases and sales of goods and services to satisfy given ends. The ideal economic agent may appear to be no more than a useful theoretical abstraction, a construct that can be used to build a representation of the economy which can then be compared to reality. But in fact economists believe that rational economic man is an accurate portrayal of the most essential forms of human behaviour and that economic policies should therefore be based directly on the theories built up from the ideal economic agent.

The economics profession has in recent years adopted the term 'agent' as its preferred description of the economic individual as part of its unceasing attempts to make the discipline appear more scientific by the adoption of 'objective' terminology. The term describes the depersonalised human who turns the wheels of the economic machine. An agent is one who acts on behalf of another. The other, on whose behalf the agent acts, is the economic system itself and the criteria of behaviour are the 'preference orderings' and 'consumption functions' invented by economists.

The extraordinary nature of the rational economic agent is recognised by some of the more critical economists as a sort of Nietzschean Superagent. Thus

> the agent has complete, fully ordered preferences (defined over the domain of the consequences of his feasible actions), perfect information and immaculate computing power[4].

But despite sustained criticism of 'rational economic man', occasionally even from within the discipline, *homo economicus* remains firmly entrenched. The implications of toppling the concept would be too overwhelming for neoclassical economics to contemplate. Fortunately for economics the basic ideal of rational economic man can be moulded so that it incorporates some additional aspects of the world which influence economic decision making, most notably risk, the costs of gathering information, and expectations about the reaction of others to one's decisions (leading to the use of game theory). But the model remains essentially one in which separate, distinct agents make autonomous decisions about the external world.

Much of this book is devoted to exploring the implications of this assumption.

The indifference curve shows how economics defines its central problem as one of how individuals maximise an 'objective function' which expresses personal trade-offs between different goods subject to constraints, in particular the income constraint. It is to no avail to attack this essentially utilitarian method by suggesting that it fails to account for non-economic motives such as nationalism or charity. It is easy, on the face of it, to extend the model to incorporate the 'ethical' preferences of individuals so that the economic agent can trade off use of more expensive plantation-grown timber for a clear conscience. The essential distortion of the economists' way of constructing the world lies in the very construction of the individual and the relationship of individuals to their world rather than in the content or the logic of the individual's preferences. This is the most important point. In essence, the human agent is reduced by economics to a repository of instrumentalist desires which generate a series of actions; these actions result in quanta of happiness, a thing which is deposited into the place occupied by the individual. As we will see, the model of *homo economicus* has been applied to the broad range of human activities, with some bizarre results.

> Furthermore, granted that de gustibus non [est] disputandum [there is no disputing tastes], this modest base is enough to ground a full-blown social theory on a model of agency which can be exported to other social sciences. . . . The satisfaction of individual preferences, aided by felicific calculation is what makes the social world go round. Social relations become instrumental in the sense that they embody exchanges in the service of individual preferences. For instance, marriage has been analysed in this spirit as an arrangement to secure mutual benefit of exchange between two agents with different endowments. Crime has been claimed to occur because calculations of costs and benefits proves it to be the action which maximises expected utility. . . . Government policies are explained on the hypothesis that the political arena is also peopled by individuals maximizing expected utility, who form coalitions to market policies which will secure reelection. In this sort of way *homo economicus* turns into a universal *homo sapiens*[5].

The Chicago economist Gary Becker puts the extreme case for the universal applicability of *homo economicus.*

> I have come to the position that the economic approach is a comprehensive one that is applicable to all human behavior. . . . Needless to say, the economic approach has not provided equal insight into and understanding of *all* kinds of behavior: for example, the determinants of war and of many other political decisions have not yet been much illuminated by this approach (or by any other approach). I believe, however, that the limited success is mainly the result of limited effort and not lack of relevance[6].

Becker's analysis of marriage will be examined next. While Becker's views may be regarded as extreme even by some economists, his position is a very logical extension of textbook economic theory to other areas of individual choice.

THE IMPERIALIST INTENT OF ECONOMICS

The infiltration of the economic way of thinking, especially into universities and public policy institutions, has almost reached saturation point. As it has spread, the utilitarian 'morality' of economic calculation has driven ethically based positions into discredit. Now we see the calculus of utility being applied to areas of life that were previously thought of as social and moral; we see economic principles applied to public education, art and culture, drug addiction, marriage, child bearing and politics itself. The foremost advocate of the colonisation of all human behaviour by economics has been Gary Becker.

Although some economists would distance themselves from Becker's work, it is difficult to argue with his claim that the application of economics to areas of human behaviour such as marriage, child bearing, crime and drug addiction is no more than a logical extension of the principles of economics—those of maximising behaviour, market equilibrium and stable preferences. Dissenting economists must specify the point at which they believe the economic approach breaks down. Let us look then at Becker's economic analysis of marriage[7].

Becker begins by suggesting that 'the neglect of marriage by economists is either a major oversight or persuasive evidence of the limited scope of economic analysis'. He sets out to rectify the oversight. Marriage is defined as an arrangement to secure the mutual benefit of exchange between two agents of different endowments. Essentially, two people marry because they expect to raise their levels of utility by doing so. This is possible because it is more efficient to produce 'household commodities' in multiple-member households. These household commodities include 'the quality of meals, the quality and quantity of children, prestige, recreation, companionship, love, and health status'.

Thus, argues Becker, 'persons in love can reduce the cost of frequent contact and of resource transfers between each other by sharing the same household'. But the analysis must go deeper:

> Economies of scale may be secured by joining households, but two or more males or females could equally well take advantage of these economies and do so when they share an apartment and cooking. Consequently, the explanation of why men and women live together must go beyond economies of scale.

The answer lies in the desire to have 'own children'. The difficulty of identifying the father in polygynous unions along with the numerical equality of the sexes make monogamous unions the most efficient form of marriage. This is why monogamy is so popular. Of course, in a monogamous marriage (and any other form of marriage), the prospective partners must calculate the returns. 'The gain from marriage has to be balanced against the costs, including legal fees and the cost of searching for a mate, to determine whether marriage is worthwhile.' The marriage market is assumed to be in equilibrium 'in the sense that no person could change mates and become better off'.

Next, Becker considers the 'effect of "love" and caring between mates on the nature of equilibrium in the marriage market'. Love can be considered to be a 'nonmarketable household commodity'. If a person loves another this increases the amount of 'caring' behaviour he or she will engage in. A marriage with more caring generates more utility for the partners because the costs of 'policing' the marriage are reduced. 'Policing is necessary in any partnership or corporation' and in the case of the marriage partnership policing 'reduces the probability that a mate shirks duties or appropriates more output than is mandated by the equilibrium in the marriage market'. Therefore, since love produces more efficient marriages, 'love and caring between two persons increase their chances of being married to each other'. In Chapter 10 of his book, Becker analyses the decision to have children in terms of the quantity and quality of children. In particular, he suggests that 'the negative relation between quantity and quality often observed is a consequence of a low substitution elasticity in a family's utility function between parents' consumption and level of living and that of their children'. This extraordinary statement seems to mean that parents of many children have 'low quality' children because they do not make big enough sacrifices to improve the quality of their children. Later he observes: 'Of course, most of our discussion applies not only to the interaction between the quantity and quality of children, but also to the quantity and quality of cars, houses, food, tea, education, publications, and large numbers of other goods'.

Becker was awarded the 1992 Nobel Prize in economics for this and related work. At one point Becker comments: 'Most people no doubt find the concept of a market allocation of commodities to beloved mates strange and unrealistic'. The archetypal economic agent defined by modern economic text books is entirely consistent with Becker's analysis. There is no reason to believe that the forms of behaviour analysed by Gary Becker and other economists—including drug addiction, crime, political behaviour, war, and racial discrimination—somehow stand outside of the rules of rational, calculating behaviour laid down in the text books.

To most people Becker's analysis of marriage will seem so fanciful that it needs no explicit criticism—its absurdity is too obvious. The most revealing and disturbing fact is that the economics profession chose to award this work its highest accolade. It will be enough here to comment briefly on the conception of humans that underlies it. In Becker's marriage market the individual confronts a set of commodities— potential husbands and wives—each with its own characteristics. The consumer must calculate the net utility to be had from exploiting the differences in endowments—physical attractiveness, earning power, degree of caring behaviour, ability to sire or bear children of the desired quality. The decision becomes one of calculation of personal benefits and costs. It would seem that Romeo and Juliet did not inherit the preference orderings of their families. There is no place for emotions that cannot be quantified and factored into the equation. We will look in vain for the passion that overwhelms reason and takes possession of the lover. Marriages in Becker's world are made not in Heaven but in the bazaar, not in the heart but in the head. Most people would find anyone who approached marriage in this way thoroughly repellant. Any counsellor will testify that marriages agreed upon on the basis of calculation of the benefits and costs would most probably be doomed, at least in the West. It might be argued that traditional arranged marriages in India, for instance, display all of the features of the Becker marriage market, but it would be an odd reversal indeed to maintain that Indians are more akin to *homo economicus* than, say, North Americans.

We must, however, ask ourselves this question: if Becker's conceptualisation of the calculating economic agent is absurd in the context of the decision to marry, in what circumstances is it not absurd? The next chapter will have much to say about the application of the neoclassical framework to environmental issues. To drive home the folly of imposing the worldview of *homo economicus* on decisions involving ethical judgements let us imagine a choice facing an Aboriginal community in the Northern Territory of Australia. Following white settlement, the community has largely disintegrated culturally; it is unable to sustain itself and most people rely on social security payments. The community is racked by alcoholism, poverty, disease and, above all, an unrelenting hopelessness. The last vestiges of self-respect derive from their ancient spiritual attachment to the land. A mining company wants to mine a sacred site. The government must decide whether national welfare will be maximised by mining or by not mining (and perhaps granting land rights to the traditional owners).

Faced with this situation the solution of economics is to put a price on the sacred site so that a comparison can be made between the spiritual value of the site and the value of the minerals. The economist asks the Aborigines if they would be willing to accept $1000 each per year for 10 years in compensation for the mining of their sacred site. They decline. Would they accept $1500? No. But the price goes up and the Aborigines begin to think about what the money could buy, perhaps a new truck, and how the money might allow a visit to some distant relatives. Perhaps they could move into a house in town to escape the desperation, or build a community centre to try to reestablish some social cohesion. Besides, whites always seem to get what they want anyway. So the Aborigines relent and the sacred site is dug up. The economist has found an amount of money which establishes the point of 'indifference' between mining, with 'compensation', and no mining. But the Aborigines feel sad; they feel impoverished in a way that no amount of money can compensate for. In the economic worldview, however, the Aborigines have exercised their free will and made a choice; they have placed a value on their sacred site. The market has spoken.

The economist might analyse the operation of the market as in Figure 2.

The indifference curve shows combinations of sacred sites and money which provide equal amounts of utility to the Aborigines. With the given budget constraint, the community can maximise its welfare at the point of tangency, T. This may seem far-fetched, even 'strange and unrealistic' in Becker's words, but if love can become a commodity there is no reason why spiritual attachments cannot also. The economist would argue that the Aborigines had a choice and made a decision; therefore they compared money values with the value to them

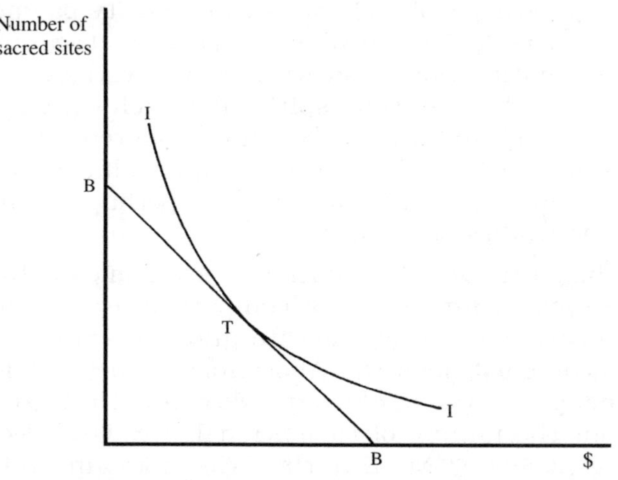

Figure 2 The point of indifference between dollars and sacred sites

of the sacred site. If they had chosen to forgo the money and keep the sacred site then that would mean that they implicitly put a higher value on the sacred site, perhaps even an infinite value. Nevertheless, in the world of economic reasoning, the act of choice means that the commensurability of all things is established. By this line of reasoning, *all* behaviour becomes subject to the economist's utilitarian calculus. It is apparent how starting with the concept of *homo economicus* defines the problem in a very particular way, one that is often wholly inappropriate.

We all make choices of material consumption over aesthetic qualities such as traditional attachments and environmental beauty. We are often left feeling sad, somehow deprived, although the connection between our decision and our sadness may not be apparent. Very often, we do not understand the biophysical connections between our decisions to consume material goods and the destruction of Nature that results. Until recently, even if we understood it, we felt powerless to stop it. Moreover, we push into our unconscious minds our intuitive understanding of the essential value to ourselves as beings of things like the existence of wilderness, a living environment, a sense of community and our links to the collective spirit. The economist within all of us—the selfish calculator—struggles with our ethical selves and, far too often, wins.

Once we understand this, the economic idea of rational choice under conditions of 'perfect knowledge' becomes a partial and tendentious conception indeed. Economics takes it as given that we are fully cognizant of the consequences for ourselves and for others of our decisions, or that the costs of acquiring the necessary information are too great to justify the anticipated benefit. But we are often unaware of outcomes, or choose not to recognise them. When we consider today the effects of smoking, working with asbestos, heavy dependence on fossil fuels or clearing the Amazon forests, we know that many of our decisions in the past have been contrary to our own interests. Yet these are not simply questions of inadequate information; our assessment of information and thus our decisions are conditioned by our attitudes, and our attitudes are socially determined. The stock of freely available information about the health effects of cigarette smoking has changed little in twenty years, but for a long time that information had no impact. In the West, smoking is now declining as more people change their attitudes about the social acceptability of smoking. Whereas smoking was once accepted as sophisticated, energetic and worldly, now it is seen as dirty, weak-willed and self-destructive.

Attitudes make us more or less receptive to information so that the 'cost' of acquiring information is not the only influence on how much information we use in making our decisions. The distinction between attitudes and information is uncomfortable for economists and they prefer to dismiss it. Two esteemed US economists, Gary Becker once again and George Stiglitz doubt that there is a distinction to be drawn between persuasive and informative advertising. In a beautiful piece of sophistry, they claim that the simplest fact about a product can be highly persuasive and the most bizarre claims for a product may contain some factual information. This is itself a bizarre claim; its purpose as always is to sustain the belief that whatever consumers choose in the free market is beyond criticism.

The knowledge that the economist attributes to the consumer at the moment of choice is knowledge at the shallowest level. There are deeper forms of knowledge, some of them unconscious, which influence our decisions. It may be that the bringing to consciousness of deeper knowledge will have a profound influence on people's consumption choices. This is why the first step towards overcoming addictions—to alcohol, cigarettes, hard drugs, food, gambling, consumer credit and so on—is to understand what it is in our lives that we are trying to satisfy. We must look beyond the instant of expressed market preferences. It is pointless to argue that alcoholics drink because alcohol makes them feel good, not least because many of them want to stop drinking. The bringing to consciousness of deeper knowledge helps to explain why increasing numbers of people are forgoing the trappings of consumerism for a life less hostile to the natural environment. This explains why some people who have experienced 'enlightenment', to use the Eastern mystical term, or have gone through a mid-life crisis may completely change their consumption patterns without any addition to their stock of 'information'.

Finally, the economist's archetypal consumption decision ignores a most fundamental feature of economic decision making in reality—power, and the inequality of power that goes with the inequality of the distribution of wealth. The stock reply of economists when confronted with the fact that a certain course of action, such as an investment proposal, will favour the rich is to claim that questions of distribution are outside of their field. Governments reflect society's distributional preferences through the tax system so that, after tax, everyone 'deserves' what they get. This subterfuge is carried on even though we all know that power is wielded very unequally in our society and that there are binding limits on redistribution. Money is power speaking. To return to our example of the picnic spot under threat of sand mining, if the picnic spot is heavily patronised by wealthy people then they will be willing to pay much more than the poor to keep it. The economist's calculations comparing the financial benefits of mining with the psychic costs of losing the picnic area will show the latter costs to be much higher than would be the case if the picnic spot happened to be located in an area heavily used by the poor. The rich would keep their picnic area and the economist would have done no more than provide a gloss of economic respectability to an outcome that has a more brutal explanation, the greater political power of the rich.

THE CYBERNETIC CONSUMER

The function of consumer theory is to provide a theoretical foundation for the political commitment of economists to the efficacy of the market and the forces of free enterprise. As we have seen, modern consumer theory is a hangover from utilitarianism. Utilitarianism, although a philosophy of great influence in the 19th century, has been driven out of the social sciences with the sole exception of economics. In economics the fundamental philosophical belief remains; that the market interaction of myriad self-interested individuals will yield maximal social benefit. This is the economists' famous invisible hand, stated by its 'discoverer', Adam Smith, as follows:

> By pursuing his own interest [a man] frequently promotes that of the society more effectually than when he really intends to promote it[8].

According to a leading economist of today, Jack Hirshleifer, this 'great unifying scientific concept' is 'one of the important intellectual achievements of humanity'—along with Newton's principle of gravitation and Darwin's principle of evolution through natural selection[9].

The political doctrine of the invisible hand is of substantial psychological importance in Western society because it sublimates greed and rapaciousness beneath a veneer of social respectability. Just as the unconsciously sadistic father believes he is beating his children for their own good, and the unconsciously lascivious morals campaigner believes he has an unpleasant duty to monitor the torrent of pornography, so those engaged in exploitation of others for their own enrichment seize upon the doctrine of the invisible hand as a means of giving conscious moral sanction to their immoral activities[10].

In Hirshleifer's widely used text book, rational decision making is defined to take the following form:

> all feasible alternatives are set out, infeasible ones are rejected;
>
> all readily available information is taken into account;
>
> in light of their consequences, alternatives are ranked in order of preference; and
>
> the highest ranking alternative is chosen[11].

If this description sounds like a generic set of instructions for a computer to solve a problem then that is no accident. By defining the problem in this way, people can be fitted comfortably into the big machine. The modern economist sees the economy as a giant, complex machine like a huge, self-winding clock. There are many different parts with names like output, the money supply, capital goods, exchange rates and so on which are connected by 'rods' with names like consumption propensities, production functions and investment and money demand functions. Human behaviour is expressed in a set of variables which are definable and measurable.

The economic machine has both a built-in goal, the achievement of 'equilibrium', and a self-regulating mechanism, the interaction of supply and demand in the price-setting process. An economic system is in equilibrium when all forces are balanced and none operates to shift the system from its path. A market is in equilibrium when the amount buyers demand equals the amount sellers have to sell at the prevailing price. The notion of an equilibrium and an equilibrating mechanism fixes the character of 'economic agents' in the process, circumscribing their forms of behaviour to those that are consistent with the attainment of equilibrium.

Modern economics might thus be described as 'cybernetic economics'. Cybernetics is the science of methods of control and communication that are common to living organisms and machines. The essence of cybernetics is the goal-oriented automaticity of the systems described and this is why the same principles can be applied to machines and humans. Human cybernetic systems, such as the system that regulates our upright position when we stand on the deck of a pitching ship, are automatic or self-regulating, without the intervention of conscious human decisions. This is precisely the perspective that economics has of the human individual; once the model has been specified, there is no place for human consciousness, let alone unconscious motivation. Outcomes are dictated by the rules of the economic model. The being constructed by economics, *homo economicus*, is a sort of economic automaton whose forms of economic behaviour are captured in the parameters of an equation.

In some respects the term 'cybernetic economics' concedes much more to economics than it deserves. If economics could adopt such a perspective it would be taking a leap forward. Economic logic mostly adopts the traditional linear-causal perspective. Some economic models permit their various component equations to be solved simultaneously. They are constructed on the basis of mutual determination of the 'endogenous' variables of the system i.e. those whose values are not given but are to be determined. But the system remains the sum of its parts, the parts being the equations of the model each of which represents a determinate relationship. As Morris Berman observes:

> The cybernetic mechanism may be a more sophisticated model than the clockwork model of the seventeenth century, but it is still, in the last analysis, a mechanism[12].

The implication of the economists' definition of rationality is that the process of decision making is already defined within a rational space. No form of behaviour is possible in this space other than rational behaviour as defined by economics. Thus forms of economic behaviour that are influenced by what we will later refer to as transrational motivations, and even prerational motivations, must be stretched and distorted in such a way that they conform to the precepts of the economist's rationality. These non-rational motivations include intuition, communion with the natural environment, the 'animal spirits' stressed by Keynes that motivate business decisions, the self-expressive function of work and, above all, the guiding lessons from transcendent knowledge.

Economic analysis begins with the assumption that rational and irrational forms of behaviour can be separated, although ultimately whatever people do in the market becomes rational. Hirshleifer writes: 'rational behavior is action selected on the basis of considered thought rather than habit, prejudice or emotion'.[13] But everyday observation of the importance of non-rational or transrational influences on economic behaviour and therefore economic welfare cannot be denied. The response of economics is to take these influences on behaviour as part of the given conditions, as part of the individual's 'preference set'. A process becomes a precondition. Once preferences are taken as given, any decision can be construed as rational. 'De gustibus non est disputandum'—there is no disputing tastes. If I refuse to buy my vegetables from the local green-grocery because it is owned buy French people, and I dislike French people, then my spending behaviour remains rational to the economist because I have simply expressed my preferences. I have chosen to pay more for my vegetables so as to avoid the psychic costs of buying from the French. I am merely maximising my utility subject to the constraints imposed by my income and my bigotry. I am rational.

This circumstance is not a special case when we consider that in Western society all of our preferences are in some ways influenced by our social conditioning. In particular, the power of advertising can be used to influence our decisions to buy particular goods. When we recognize how much of our purchasing is influenced by fashion—from clothes to cars to health foods to housing and furnishing, indeed, almost everything—it is clear that a huge volume of irresistible social pressures are squashed into our 'preference sets'. Whatever we decide, whatever the influences on our decisions, our choices in the marketplace are rational in the economists' lexicon. The enormous legitimacy this conception gives to the market is apparent. Whatever outcomes the market produces are rational and therefore desirable and in some way sacrosanct; free will is given the blessing of the market and who but the arrogant or subversive could question the right of each individual to spend their money how they wish?

The economists' term for outcomes determined by consumers' preferences is consumer sovereignty; it is often used as an unchallengeable reference point when the desirability of market outcomes is questioned by critics. Whatever an individual decides based on easily accessible information is rational. None can challenge the imperious god of consumer sovereignty. When one *begins* with the individual as the essential component of analysis—an individual defined as an isolated ego interacting with a wholly external world—these conclusions follow ineluctably. When economists attack social critics of consumer sovereignty as elitists, are not the economists, whose definitions determine whether our behaviour is rational or irrational, truly the elitists?

But, it might be objected, is not the economists' definition good enough for most economic applications? As long as one is content to remain within the economists' utilitarian morality, it may be. One can then turn one's face away from the perversions and injustices that the market sometimes induces; one can entrust the future of the natural environment to the imperatives of self-interest.

Economic rationality, then, serves powerful social functions. In particular, it gives legitimacy to the power of those who speak with money. If we dislike something then we will be willing to pay to avoid it. What people do with their money expresses their rational decisions. The spending of money, the willingness to pay, becomes the touchstone by which outcomes are to be judged. In fact, as we will see, willingness to pay is the foundation stone of cost-benefit analysis, which is, more formally or less formally, the framework in which all private and public investment decisions are evaluated.

In the 1980s, the most dynamic thrust within the discipline of economics came from the Rational Expectations School. According to the theory of rational expectations, not only do individuals behave rationally in their current economic transactions, but we behave rationally over time, foreseeing the consequences of our actions for ourselves and the whole economy. In making decisions, we are thought to take into account the effects of our present actions on economic variables in the future, knowing that our present actions and those of others will influence the outcomes. We are believed to operate on the basis of determinate economic models that we unwittingly carry around in our heads. Thus we have propositions such as the 'Ricardian Equivalence Theorem' which maintains that an increase in government spending financed by borrowing from the public will have no effect on the total level of spending in the economy. This is because we, as taxpayers, understand that taxes will have to be raised in ten or twenty years time to pay off the government's debt, so we cut back our current spending and increase our savings to finance the increased taxes we will be required to pay in the future. If true, this theorem would be a relief to agencies that counsel those beset by consumer debt. Politically, the Ricardian Equivalence Theorem represented the *coup de grâce* in the Reagan-Thatcher battle against Keynesian policies of economic management through government spending. Any additional government spending will only be offset by a fall in private saving. The theorem demands a further withdrawal from collective forms of action or social control of the economy, leaving economic outcomes solely to the activities of private individuals in the market.

It is clear that the economists have captured the concept of rationality for very partial uses. It is illuminating to observe the effect of exposing someone from a culture not obsessed with the cult of rationality to Western economics. The most senior economic decision makers in some Asian countries have been trained in the United States and have very successfully absorbed the theorems of the economic worldview. But somehow the world appears different on their return home. Japan is a good case, a country which has evolved culturally and intellectually well outside of the Western tradition and has, from the perspective of the European Enlightenment, maintained an adherence to more 'primitive' conceptions of the human character and the societies formed by them. The conception of the individual in Japan bears no resemblance to that in the West and the abstractions of the economics texts remain just that, abstractions. While Western-trained Japanese economists have been highly proficient at learning the ways of economics—indeed, they tend to excel at the more arid, mathematical forms—economic policy formation in Japan has managed to go beyond the boundaries imposed by the discipline. The idea that human welfare is maximised by the unhindered expression of individual preferences in the marketplace is treated in practice as a curiosity of Western textbooks. This is in no sense as endorsement of the Japanese social system, which has been in many ways as brutal in its attitudes to the natural environment and human creativity as those of the West, but when the task is to manage an economy composed of complex people in a myriad of subtle but powerful social relationships, the 'irrational' forces excluded from the textbooks have to be incorporated into the analysis and harnessed in the pursuit of policy objectives.

CAUSATION AND THE ECONOMIC MACHINE

Nowhere is the method of 'cybernetic economics' more clearly expressed than in the use of econometrics. This statistical technique takes an economic variable, such as the demand for hogs or the level of investment, and breaks it down into its 'causal' components. For example, the demand for hogs becomes a function of the price of hogs, the price of sheep (if people substitute mutton for pork) and the incomes of people who buy hogs.

While it is acknowledged that the numerical analysis itself does not prove causation (eg. that a rise in the price of hogs reduces the demand for them), this is always the purpose of the exercise and in fact several 'tests of causality' are widely used. In econometric analysis, economic theory is first used to form a hypothesis about the relationship between the dependent variable (the one whose values are determined, the demand for hogs in our example) and the independent or causal variables (prices and income in our example). The hypothesis is then tested using statistical data. The simple-minded linear view of economic causation (practiced by some very clever people) is often made more sophisticated by the use of simultaneous equations models in which the partial interdependence of variables is built into the models. However the mechanical notion of causation remains.

An essentially Newtonian idea of causation underlies all economic work; it reflects the cybernetic view of the economy as a huge machine. When the mechanical view of the economy is abandoned in favour of an organic view, a view in which the integrity of the whole is accepted and the laws of motion of the whole system are the object of study, then new notions of causality can be entertained. As we have from birth been schooled, formally and informally, in the ideas of linear causation and the analytical method, alternative notions of causality are difficult for us to understand and accept. Nevertheless, we must begin to accept these ideas, for the limits of linear causality have been reached. As long as we hold on to the mechanical model of the world our own level of awareness and development will both individually and collectively be constrained.

Fritjof Capra argues that the conceptual breakthroughs that led to the emergence of quantum physics suggest the idea of *nonlocal causation.*

> The fundamental role of nonlocal connections and of probability in atomic physics implies a new notion of causality that is likely to have profound implications for all fields of science. Classical science was constructed by the Cartesian method of analyzing the world into parts and arranging those parts according to causal laws. . . . Quantum theory has shown us that the world cannot be analyzed into independently existing isolated elements[14].

In quantum theory an individual event does not always have a well-defined cause in the sense that one can point to a local event that is responsible for it. But this does not mean that these events occur at random, without a cause, only that their causes are not local.

> The behaviour of any part is determined by its nonlocal connections to the whole, and since we do not know these connections precisely, we have to replace the narrow classical notion of cause and effect by the wider concept of statistical causality.[15]

In a system characterised by nonlocal causation, the concepts and laws of the whole explain the behaviour of the parts of the system. This is completely contrary to the method of classical mechanics in which the properties of the parts determine those of the whole system. The biologist Rupert Sheldrake has challenged the mechanical idea of gene-based evolution with the new idea of morphic fields. Living organisms (and non-living things like crystals) are influenced not only by the genes they inherit but by morphic fields. Morphic fields are invisible realms of influence around and within organisms that contain the memory of the experiences and characteristics of pre-existing organisms of the same type. A developing organism comes under the influence of the morphic fields of its species and is shaped by the collective memory of the species. It thus inherits both genes (by a process of mechanical transmission) and morphic fields. The latter are passed on non-materially by a process Sheldrake calls morphic resonance, 'the influence of like upon like through space and time'.

> Morphic resonance does not fall off with distance. It does not involve a transfer of energy, but of information. In effect, this hypothesis enables the regularities of nature to be understood as governed by habits inherited by morphic resonance, rather than by eternal, nonmaterial, and nonenergetic laws[16].

Sheldrake cites a range of experimental evidence from, for example, the formation of crystals and the development of fruit flies that lends weight to the hypothesis[17].

Recognising the limitations of linear causation in the mechanical tradition, Carl Jung put forward the notion of *synchronicity* in order to understand certain observed psychological phenomena. The notions of synchronicity and nonlocal causation are similar. The psychotherapist Peter O'Connor writes that

> we have inherited and hold in our psyche the model of linear causality (that is, if something happens it must have had a cause!) and if no reason can be discovered then most people will simply conclude that we do not yet know *the* cause. . . . Jung developed the idea of synchronicity as an additional model or alternative model or explanation for certain phenomena . . . . Synchronicity simply means that some things co-occur, so-called coincidentally and not in a linear causal fashion.[18]

When we begin to think about alternatives to the traditional perception of linear causation we are inclined to abandon the conceited idea that we can conquer the world by understanding it. In the mechanical view, we understand the world by separating ourselves from it, when indeed the deepest knowledge is had by immersing ourselves in it. We can really understand some of the great truths only by actively breaking down the barriers that we set up between ourselves and our worlds, beginning with that stubborn, deluding barrier called ego. The knowledge that comes from breaking down the barriers includes the day-to-day intuitive understanding that can be had from direct relationships with nature and with other people.

The idea that we can conquer the world by analyzing it is precisely the attitude of economics. To be sure, some concede that there may be a few fuzzy edges to the machine. These show themselves in the form of the 'error term' of econometric calculations, the random element that cannot quite be eliminated. But the all-pervasive view remains that if only the model can be perfected and the data purified then true understanding of the economic machine can be revealed.

Hirshleifer, like the profession in general, displays a faith in the advancement of social welfare through scientific discovery which has all the wide-eyed naivety of the 19th-century utilitarians.

> When economists disagree on policy issues, it may be because they are seeking divergent goals ... But it is often the case that variance of opinion among economists is over *means* rather than *goals*. Further scientific progress in positive economics will, over time, tend to eliminate the source of disagreement.[19]

THE SANCTITY OF MARKETS

We have seen that the starting point of modern economic analysis is individual choice in the marketplace. In the economists' market, an individual in the possession of goods or services confronts another individual in the possession of money or other goods and exchange takes place. Each individual has a clear set of rules for the conduct of the process leading to exchange. The interaction is devoid of any influence other than rational calculation aimed at maximising personal welfare.

Prices in the marketplace provide the rule for determining the value of goods for individuals. Microeconomic theory 'proves' market prices to be an expression of consumers' marginal preferences. In other words, in competitive markets actual prices assume the levels they do because they show the trade-offs people are willing to make between one good and others. Because prices are 'proved' to be the expression of the free will of consumers, they are sacrosanct. Free markets then become an untouchable adjunct to liberal democracy.

Since free will is expressed in markets and markets generate prices, when economists are faced with problems of public policy their natural inclination is to turn to the price mechanism. There is an immediate presupposition that social and economic problems must be due to the failure of markets to work properly and the implication is that there are some impediments, probably imposed by a government, to the untrammelled expression of individual free will.

The economic way of thinking and the direct relationship between prices and welfare can be revealed by examining the assumptions underlying cost-benefit analysis. Cost-benefit analysis encapsulates the essential precepts of economics. It should be pointed out, however, that cost-benefit analysis was developed as a tool of government policy to be applied when private markets fail and cannot be made to work. It is an attempt to anticipate or reproduce the outcome that markets would produce if they could be made to work. As we will see in the next chapter there are economists who will not even condone cost-benefit analysis as it requires the government to collect and analyze information and then to make a decision based on it. For these ultra-free market believers, the role of government is not to make any resource allocation decisions but only to provide the legal framework in which unfettered markets allocate resources.

As an example of cost-benefit analysis we take an analysis of a project designed to reforest a severely deforested area of the Himalayan foothills in Nepal. It is a 'social forestry' or 'community forestry' project, as opposed to a commercial logging operation, in that the products of the forest are destined wholly for harvest and consumption by local villagers in their household and farming activities. The project is a sort of reverse illustration of the kind of debate that rages between logging companies and environmentalists over the value of logging. Here we are evaluating the net economic benefits of reestablishing trees rather than cutting them down.

Nevertheless, the economic assumptions and methods are the same.

While the economic issues involved in growing trees and in cutting them down are identical, the social and environmental issues are, of course, entirely different. If economists ignore the social and environmental implications of forestry operations, as indeed they generally do, then it is irrelevant whether the proposed investment involves reforestation or deforestation. The management of forest resources is simply a matter of maximising the gains, expressed in monetary form, from competing land uses. If importance is attached to the social and environmental effects then reforestation and deforestation become very different forms of investment.

The first task of the project evaluator is to identify all of the 'economic' costs and benefits. The costs of the reforestation project examined here are those of employing the labour of foresters, planters, builders of nurseries, and nursery workers as well as the costs of purchasing cement, seeds, poly-pipe, tools and so on needed to build nurseries and to plant trees. The benefits take the form of the products of the newly established forests—fuelwood for cooking and heating, fodder for cattle and timber for village construction—which flow for many years after the start of the project.

The next step is to attach prices to all of the costs and benefits. The prices employed may need to be 'shadow prices' which are measures of true market prices where actual market prices either do not exist or are 'distorted' by government intervention or market imperfections. The costs are easy to put prices on because they mostly take the form of money spent. The benefits, however, are forest products which are consumed directly by local village users and not marketed as commodities. Various ingenious methods are available to attach shadow prices to a tonne of fuelwood or a head-load of fodder. Attaching money values to the benefits is the critical stage of the cost-benefit analysis because it allows us to add up the costs and benefits and arrive at the total net benefits or the rate of return of the investment. A monetary stream of net benefits is calculated and can, after being suitably discounted over time (a subject discussed below), be compared to the net benefits of an alternative project competing for the investment funds to determine which project represents the best value for money.

The assignment of prices to the costs and benefits of the project carries with it the crucial idea that we are attaching consumers' 'preferences' to the various costs and benefits. This is the most important principle underlying cost-benefit analysis. Since the whole purpose is to decide which investment will most improve 'welfare' (the sum of material goods available to people), some means is required to translate outputs of a project into improvements in welfare. The use of prices (whether actual or shadow prices) as the appropriate measures of welfare is deduced from the operation of markets. If a person is willing to pay $1 for a kilo of rice and $1 for a T-shirt then a kilo of rice must confer as much utility or welfare improvement on that person as one T-shirt. If the operation of the markets for rice and T-shirts determines these prices then these prices represent society's comparative valuations of a kilo of rice and a T-shirt. The concept of willingness to pay is really quite essential because it gives social sanction to the outcomes that markets generate. The question of the distinction between *willingness* to pay and *ability* to pay is generally deemed irrelevant because everyone is considered to have the income that they deserve. The income each person deserves is that which other markets confer by setting prices for the services (especially the labour services and the 'services' provided by capital) that individuals decide to offer at the going price. It is a wonderful construction.

One dollars' worth of fuelwood provides as much utility as one dollars' worth of fodder, or indeed as much utility as one dollars' worth of tobacco or rice. The more sensitive cost-benefit analyst may decide to introduce income distribution into the analysis by assigning a higher 'social valuation' to the consumption of poor people (for example by using the technique developed by Squire and van der Tak at the World Bank). But this does not alter the fundamental assumption underlying economic evaluation: the more dollars returned by a project—even after these dollars have been shadow priced, socially weighted and appropriately discounted—measures greater net output of goods and more utility. These goods are poured into the passive human receptacle to generate utility. The project chosen will be the one that generates more utility or welfare than the alternatives. And it is precisely through the method of cost-benefit analysis described above that many decisions regarding public investment are made. The reforestation project described above was approved by the Ministry of Finance because an economist could come up with prices that showed that the project was an efficient way to spend money—it had a rate of return of 10 per cent, just high enough to make it 'worthwhile'.

But, as everyone except the economic rationalist knows, there are some things, crucial things, missing from even the best cost-benefit analysis. When one considers the integral part played by forests in the hill communities of Nepal, and the cycle of economic and social reproduction of which they are an essential part, then it becomes clear that the project in question is not one to be determined by relative prices. At one level it is about supplying basic needs for food, warmth and housing which are not things people 'prefer' to have one over another. At another level the project is about changing social patterns, political power, both locally and nationally, and about preserving or transforming a way of life and the relationships people have to their natural environment and to each other. What is the price to be attached to taking control of forests away from the central government and putting it in the hands of villagers? What is the price of enhancing the influence of women in decision making over the use of forest resources and the household implications of this? In fact these were some of the real issues, but those who held the purse strings were concerned only with the net present dollar value of the flows of material costs and benefits.

Above all, economic analysis turns everything into relative values measured by money. There is no room for ethics. Ethical principles are absolutes. In economics, once preferences are given, there are no absolutes—there are only relativities. The only question is the price of one good relative to the price of another. Absolutes like ethical principles, social justice, political power and personal relationships can play no legitimate role. In reality, ethical considerations underlie almost all government decisions concerning the allocation of funds. All decisions have an impact on the distribution of income and most forms of investment affect the natural environment significantly. But these considerations have been subsumed in the economists' calculations on the assumption that people's ethical beliefs will somehow find expression in the relative prices they pay for goods in markets.

The notion of *right behaviour* underlies a great deal of human behaviour, including economic behaviour. For most people, a decision on whether an action is morally right or wrong precedes any calculation of the economic costs and benefits of the action. The calculated economic benefits may exceed the costs yet the action in question may remain wrong. If someone derives pleasure from pulling the wings off butterflies, their utility probably exceeds the disutility of others who are not affected. Most people, however, regard pulling the wings off butterflies as immoral or at least as undesirable behaviour. It contravenes our social norms. Indeed, the more pleasure the person derives from pulling the wings off butterflies the more repugnant to most people the act becomes. We have laws against many forms of behaviour that are regarded as unethical.

In these circumstances it would be a perverse question indeed to ask how much people would be willing to pay to compensate others for their loss of pleasure if they were prevented from pulling the wings off butterflies. Most people would be uncomprehending if asked such a question; but on reflection they might say that they would not be willing to pay anything. They would, however, strongly support legislation outlawing cruelty to animals. If pressed, these people would probably agree that some things are appropriately valued by private market behaviour while others are properly community decisions made using moral criteria, perhaps in addition to economic costs and benefits. Economists often argue that people cannot have a strong moral objection to something— such as an environmentally damaging development, cruel farming practices or a high death toll on the highways— because they have not changed their economic behaviour to reflect such views. The fact that people appear to behave inconsistently by attaching lower private market values than their social or ethical values seem to imply is no grounds for concluding that social or ethical values are in fact weak. The connection made by economists between private market behaviour and social and ethical concerns is not made by most ordinary people. For example, the fact that people do not fully recycle their waste does not mean they do not care about the environment. They may feel that they want to compensate for their private behaviour by supporting the government in measures to protect the environment, measures that may compel them to recycle. The fact that we do not take out life insurance against our children does not mean that we do not value their lives. Indeed, the decision not to take out life insurance may be an affirmation that their lives are outside the realm of monetary valuation. The act of putting a price on some things actually cheapens them in our estimation.[20]

We will see in the next chapter how contingent valuation surveys create hypothetical markets for 'public goods' such as environmental preservation. They attempt through surveys of the public to 'put a price on the environment'. Some people respond to being asked how much they would be willing to pay to protect the environment by declaring that environmental protection is a government responsibility rather than a question of payment by private citizens. The better contingent valuation surveys have a question designed to pick up these responses. The problem is to know what to do with them. They cannot be ignored, for they are valid responses reflecting genuine political or ethical views. The utilitarian calculus of the economists runs up against the issue of moral rights or right behaviour ('non-utilitarian values'). We are left with two incommensurable effects, economic and moral, and the solution cannot be found in more complete application of prices but only in deliberative reflection on the part of ourselves as moral philosophers and citizens. Economics simply cannot incorporate these values without doing violence to our beliefs. Even within market capitalist societies *homo economicus* cannot be a universal representation of humankind because, praise be, we are inescapably moral beings as well as economic agents.

Decisions about the environment are heavily laden with these ethical issues—the right to clean air, the ethics of species preservation, the integrity of ecosystems, the inviolability of sacred sites, and so on. They cannot be avoided and they cannot be reduced to monetary valuation no matter how clever the economic techniques. While they have economic implications, they simply are not economic questions. Today, as the health of the global ecosystem declines cumulatively, almost every economic decision has significant environmental effects. Exclusive reliance on economic solutions can only lead to disaster.

THE ENVIRONMENTALIST CHALLENGE

For many people, the attempt to transform all things into relative values that can be measured by dollars is most disturbing in the case of decisions affecting the natural environment. The agenda of the new environmental economics is discussed in detail in the next chapter. Here we confine ourselves to but one of the most glaring demonstrations of the incommensurability of the natural environment and the 'goods' of the economists—the use of discount rates in making decisions affecting the environment.

The discount rate is the obverse of the interest rate and captures the idea that, other things being equal, people prefer to consume now rather than later. Thus if I ask whether you would prefer to have $100 now or $100 in a year's time, most would say 'now'. If I ask whether you would prefer $90 now or $100 in a year, you might reconsider but still prefer the money now. When I ask whether you would prefer $80 now or $100 in a year some would take $100 in a year. The rate of conversion you choose is said to express your 'rate of time preference'. When this idea is applied to a stream of monetary benefits, it is clear that $100 worth of benefits that accrue well into the future will have a much lower present value than $100 worth of benefits that could be had immediately. For example, using an annual discount rate of 10 per cent, the present value of $100 accruing in 20 years time is only $14.90. Thus when an economist puts a monetary value on an 'environmental good' (and there are many clever ways of doing this), the 'present value' of the benefits it generates over time will be very small since the main benefits of the environmental good will not accrue for many years into the future.

We are familiar with the idea of a *private* discount rate because it corresponds to the interest rate our savings earn in a bank. The social discount rate is the rate at which future costs and benefits are discounted in public investment projects or private projects with a 'social' component. It is used by governments when assessing the returns to 'society' of a particular investment project. The social discount rate is considered to be a better measure of *society's* rate of time preference than the private interest rate, but it contains within it many of the contradictions of economics. The social discount rate is a theoretical construct rather than an observable product of market forces. Thus unlike the private interest rate which can be said to be the practical expression of the choices of myriad individuals, the social discount rate explicitly makes 'inter-personal utility comparisons', viz. that this person's consumption choices over time are the same as that persons' so that we can add up everyone's time preferences to arrive at a social discount rate which expresses 'society's' preference for current over future consumption.

The iconoclastic but respectable economist A. K. Sen summarises the usual arguments for constructing a social discount rate for use by governments to assess investment projects rather than simply using the private interest rate thrown up by financial markets.[21] They are:

(1) The super-responsibility argument: the government has responsibility not merely to the current generation but also to future generations (over and above the concern for future generations already reflected in the market behaviour of the present generation). Private markets express the selfish behaviour of the current generation.

(2) The dual-role argument: the members of the present generation in their political or public role may be more concerned about the welfare of future generations than they are in their day-to-day market activities. In other words, as private economic agents people think and behave differently compared to their behaviour as citizens.

(3) The isolation argument: members of the present generation may be willing to join in a collective contract of more savings by all, though unwilling to save more in isolation. So, for example, people are willing to pay more in taxes if they know that everyone else has to pay too.

Each of these arguments suggests that the social discount rate used to calculate the benefits to society of alternative investments (as opposed to the benefits to private individuals) will be lower than the private discount rate. If it is lower then projects which have large environmental benefits that flow for many years into the future will tend to be favoured over those that do not preserve the natural environment but encourage rapid depletion of resources. It remains true, however, that the use of a positive social discount rate always means that the present value of the natural environment declines over time, and after a period of 50 years will generally be insignificant.

To the extent that decisions about the natural environment involve moral choices—and surely the condition in which we leave the natural world for future generations is one of the weightiest moral choices—discounting can only cloud the issue. For many people, a healthy environment in fifty or a hundred years time is just as valuable as a healthy environment now, perhaps more so. When we earn interest on our savings this may well reflect our private discounting behaviour. But for many people the idea of discounting the future with respect to the natural environment does not make sense. The environment can be discounted like other goods only if it can be treated as conceptually identical to other goods, i.e. that the environment consists of a collection of 'goods' or 'resources' for which there are demands and supplies and thus money prices. Once money prices are attached this means that environmental goods are entirely commensurable with other types of goods and can be bought and sold in exactly the same way as we buy groceries at the local supermarket. But people do not think of the environment as a collection of goods. The idea of attaching prices to the environment or aspects of it appears strange, indeed abhorrent, even if choices do have to be made between preserving the environment and exploiting it for financial gain. The fact is that the idea of the natural environment as something that generates a stream of services for human consumption, a stream that can be discounted to give a 'present value', runs contrary to many people's moral sensibilities.

The economic decisions of governments—over matters like the clearing of tropical forests, the mining of areas of natural beauty, the dumping of toxic wastes into the sea—reflect and determine the type of society in which we live. Sometimes the most profound ethical values lie at the heart of these decisions. The instrumentalism of the economists—which assesses the values of things only so far as they satisfy our 'needs', that is the needs of isolated individuals who live separate from the world—cannot permit definitions of 'value' other than the economic one. Utilitarianism becomes the enemy of morality. Ethical values exist at a different level of quality. Very often, an ethical decision must be made prior to any economic analysis.

The ethical imperative of leaving a sacred site undisturbed or of protecting a species from extinction may render the concept of economic value irrelevant. Most economists are alarmed when it is suggested that we may decide not even to assess the economic value of a mine or a dam, for no matter what the capacity of the resource to generate material wealth, it cannot match the spiritual wealth of its natural state.

It would not be correct to maintain a rigid contrast between economic motivations and ethical ones because 'economic' behaviour often has important moral aspects. The morality of a decision rarely lies exclusively on one side of the debate. For instance, while preserving a species whose habitat is threatened by logging is an ethical issue, the unemployment and social disruption that a ban on logging might bring about is also an ethical issue. However, the methods of economics are capable of capturing neither type of ethical issue, although this has not prevented economists from attempting to 'measure' social disruption by the financial compensation people would be willing to accept for losing their jobs or the 'psychic cost' of species loss by the amount people would be willing to pay to avoid it.

To the Philistine economist this emphasis on the ethical values of decisions may be mystical bunk. So it is to the business people who exploit the natural environment for its money value. They and their hired economists—and, it must be conceded, the economist within each of us—are driven by instrumentalist self-interest and the ideology of economics that justifies it. The tragic error of economics, and of ourselves when we allow ourselves to be possessed by *homo economicus*, is to believe that the selfish calculator is *all* that we are. By separating the economy from the rest of society, by separating the economic forms of human behaviour from the totality of the person, and by constructing an economic individual—*homo economicus*—with well-defined and measurable modes of behaviour, economics thinks it has created the universal economic being. *Homo economicus* knows no national borders and is used just as comfortably as a method of analysing the arbitrage of Wall Street, the cocaine trade of Columbia, the kibbutzim of Israel, or the barter economies of the New Guinea Highlands. Anthropologists, many of whom are disillusioned economists, despair at the arrogance of the assumption of homogeneity that is visited by the economists upon diverse cultures.

It has already been suggested that the Newtonian conception of the economy as a giant machine means that cybernetic economics cannot capture the complex and subtle reality of human desire, motivation and behaviour. Even in our economic forms of behaviour we are often driven by obscure and powerful forces that are wholly unrelated to the surface appearances that are the exclusive focus of economics. The clever salesperson can recognise and exploit those subtle motivations that cannot be found in the mechanical formulations of the economics books. Advertisers communicate messages that appeal to our self-ideals and attach images, often subconscious ones, to products that have nothing whatever to do with the functions actually served by them.

Preoccupied with consumption for consumption's sake, economics is confined to the analysis of surface appearances, the expression in the marketplace of our collective neuroses, and this only serves to conceal the things that can really give us fulfilled lives. But, it might be argued, can economics do any more than that? Economists are not psychoanalysts; can they be expected to delve into the deepest motivations and sources of gratification of the human animal in order to understand economic behaviour? It is true that economists are not psychologists; but it is not true that economics has no psychology. For all of its claims to value-free analysis, economics is founded on a definite though rarely analysed perception of the psychological foundations of human behaviour. This psychology perhaps emerged most clearly in our discussion of Becker's analysis of marriage. The argument here is not for the injection of psychology into economics, but for the rebuilding of economics on a psychology that knows the true nature of humans, as individuals and as citizens, and as inseparable parts of the cosmic whole.

Economists cannot absolve themselves from responsibility; they cannot pretend that psychology does not matter. If economics claims to have a body of ideas to explain how economies work and how human welfare is advanced, if economics is willing to make recommendations about the best policies to be adopted, then it must face up to the fact that as long as its analysis is confined to surface appearances and its psychology is a false one, then its recommendations will completely miss their mark. Its assumptions about the nature of humans and the function of consumption lead it to policies that result in greater impoverishment. When we look at the personal misery that pervades Western society, and compare this with the official ideology that economic growth is the path to human happiness, the capacity for human self-delusion is frighteningly apparent.

Many people bridle at the economic conception of the individual, and it has come under particularly severe, if at times inchoate, attack from the environmental movement. The economists' individual simply does not accord with our understanding of our own personal motivations and behaviour. For example, I care for the environment and am willing to go without bleached paper in order to save the rivers and seas from pollution by chlorines. 'Easy', say the economists, 'we will simply add to your utility function a concern for the environment and let you make choices between bleached paper and pollution'. But this is not the point at all and only demonstrates the narrowness inherent in the economists' conception of the economic agent. I care for the environment as a social being not as an individual; I care for the environment ethically, not economically; I care for the environment not because its condition influences the range and quality of goods available for me to choose from (including healthy fish and pleasant scenery) but because the environment is an expression of myself. The economists' idea of the consuming subject making choices about consumable objects is an alienated one, one that robs me of my humanity. I do not *consume* environmental goods—clean air, unspoiled wilderness, native animal species, quietness—I live them. Indeed, I may never see a whale or a wilderness, but they remain part of me. And this is why millions of people who will never step outside of a metropolis now support the environmental movement. We somehow have a long-lost, primordial feeling—one that we cannot express, one that mostly remains in our unconscious minds but which influences our beliefs and behaviour—that the destruction of the environment is the destruction of ourselves. After centuries of industrial growth, scientific knowledge and intellectual development we have not, and never will, truly lose this essential part of being human. What was true for a Native American like Luther Standing Bear remains true for all of us, if only we had the divine inspiration to see it:

> We are of the soil and the soil is of us. We love the birds and the beasts that grew with us on this soil. They drank the same water as we did and breathed the same air. We are all one in nature. Believing so, there was in our hearts a great peace and a welling kindness for all living, growing things.[22]

1   The idea has a strange parallel in the way drug addicts come to see the world. Jean Liedloff writes as follows:
    'Another addict put it this way. He said that other people looked for lots of things to make them happy: love, money, power, wives, children, good looks, status, clothes, nice houses, all the rest of it, but all an addict wants is one thing, all his demands can be satisfied at once, by the drug.' *The Continuum Concept* (Gerald Duckworth & Co., London, 1975) p. 110

2   For a very cogent presentation of this argument see Steven Kelman, 'Cost-Benefit Analysis and Environmental, Safety, and Health Regulation: Ethical and Philosophical Considerations' in Daniel Swartzman (ed.), *Cost-Benefit Analysis and Environmental Regulations: Politics, Ethics, and Methods* (The Conservation Foundation, Washington D.C., 1982).

3   The economics profession sees its discipline as the emperor of the social sciences. 'The economist has allowed [sic] this division of intellectual labour to operate, leaving the explanation of the formation of tastes and goals for other social sciences.' (Jack Hirshleifer, *Price Theory and Applications*, Third Edition, Prentice-Hall, New Jersey, 1984, p. 9) Needless to say, these other social sciences are lesser social sciences.

4   Entry on 'economic man' in *The New Palgrave: A Dictionary of Economics* (Cambridge University Press, Cambridge, 1988) by Sean Hargreaves-Heap and Martin Hollis.

5   Hargreaves-Heap and Hollis in Palgraves, *ibid.*

6   Gary Becker, *The Economic Approach to Human Behavior* (University of Chicago Press, Chicago, 1976) pp. 8–9 (my emphasis)

7   Much of Gary Becker's work is reproduced in his book *The Economic Approach to Human Behavior* (University of Chicago Press, Chicago, 1976). The quotations that follow are from Chapter 11, 'A Theory of Marriage'.

8   Adam Smith, *The Wealth of Nations*, Book IV, Chapter 2

9   Hirshleifer, *op. cit.*, p. 13

10 See Erich Fromm, *Beyond the Chains of Illusion* (Simon and Schuster, New York, 1962) p. 90.

11 Hirshleifer, *op. cit.*, p. 7 *passim*

12 Morris Berman, *The Reenchantment of the World*, (Cornell University Press, Ithaca, 1981) p. 286

13 Hirshleifer, *op. cit.*, p. 8

14 Fritjof Capra, *The Turning Point* (Flamingo, London, 1983) p. 75

15 *Ibid.*, p. 76

16 Rupert Sheldrake, *The Rebirth of Nature: The Greening of Science and God* (Bantam Books, New York, 1991) p. 111. Sheldrake also stresses that Charles Darwin cannot be counted among the neo-Darwinians for whom everything depends on inherited genes. 'Darwin took it for granted that acquired characteristics could be inherited and placed great emphasis on the role of habit in the evolutionary process. He provided many examples of the hereditary effects of the habits of life. For instance, in domesticated fowls, ducks, and geese, he noted the decrease in size of wing bones and increase in size of leg bones' *(ibid.,* p. 142).

17 See also Rupert Sheldrake, *The New Science of Life: The Hypothesis of Formative Causation* (Blond & Briggs, London, 1985).

18 Peter O'Connor, *Understanding Jung, Understanding Yourself* (Methuen, North Ryde, 1985) pp. 142–143

19 Hirshleifer, *op. cit.,* p. 13

20 See Kelman, *op. cit.* Kelman also observes (p. 147): 'The willingness to pay for sex bought from a prostitute is less than the perceived value of the sex consummating love. (Imagine the reaction if a practitioner of cost-benefit analysis computed the benefits of sex in our society based on the price of prostitute services.)' In fact, Gary Becker argues that marriage is attractive only because it produces own children. 'Sexual gratification, cleaning, feeding, and other services can be purchased . . . ' (Becker, *op cit.,* p. 210)

21 A.K. Sen, *Resources, Values and Development* (Harvard University Press, 1984) p. 175

22 Luther Standing Bear, 1933, quoted in A. Booth and H. Jacobs, 'Ties That Bind: Native American Beliefs as a Foundation for Environmental Consciousness', *Environmental Ethics*, Volume 12, Number 1, Spring 1990

3 THE POVERTY OF ENVIRONMENTAL ECONOMICS

Conventional economics has traditionally paid little attention to the natural environment. Natural resources have been treated as 'factors of production' and have received less attention than the demand for and supply of the other factors of production, human labour and capital equipment. 'Resource economics' is a branch of economics that deals with the problems of non-renewable resources such as minerals, and the principal challenge is to calculate the optimal rate of depletion. It is assumed that as one resource approaches depletion the price system will ensure that substitutes are found for it. It is fair to say that traditional economics has not regarded resource depletion and environmental degradation as serious problems.

As we might expect, there was a good theoretical argument for dismissing concern about depletion of the natural environment. As a natural resource disappears or is damaged, market forces will make it profitable to exploit substitutes, so that as hardwood timber runs out its price will be driven up and that will make substitutes such as plantation softwood, steel and plastics more attractive. Moreover, the argument continues, if people are really concerned about environmental degradation due to economic activity then they will express their concern through their market behaviour. Since people have not changed their economic behaviour to protect the environment they are not really concerned about damage to it and all of the fuss is made by an unrepresentative lunatic fringe. This line of argument still pervades much of the economics profession.

The inadequacies of traditional economics became very apparent in the 1970s and 1980s. Because of the inability of economics to deal convincingly with the rash of major policy issues concerning the environment, decision-makers were forced to rely on advice based on scientific information and political considerations. It became apparent that increasing numbers of people were deeply concerned about the short and long-term implications of damage to the natural environment. Within the discipline of economics there emerged 'environmental economics' which incorporated and went beyond the old resource economics. Responding to electoral pressures, there was great interest within Western governments in new economic ways of examining and solving environmental problems. A handbook by David Pearce and his colleagues from the University of London, *Blueprint for a Green Economy*, is said have heavily influenced the conservative Thatcher Government. Many texts on environmental economics have been published in the last few years and there are even a few new professional journals devoted to the topic. Many people have invested a great deal of hope that environmental economics will provide rational solutions to our increasingly serious environmental problems.

The newer breed of environmental economists tend to be more liberal in their political views than their colleagues. This is by no means uniformly true since the area has attracted the attention of some very right wing, libertarian economists. Environmental economists usually begin by acknowledging that markets are imperfect and that consumers are not able to express their preferences for protecting the environment by means of their market activity. As a result, the values that people attach to an unspoiled wilderness or the survival of whales do not offset the commercial values of logging and whaling. We will explore the ways in which environmental economics has attempted to incorporate these values into its analysis.

In this chapter, the term 'environmental economics' refers to the application of the principles of mainstream economics to environmental issues. There is a new stream of thought emerging under the rubric of 'ecological economics' that is attempting to transcend the 'rational choice' model of economics and develop a new framework that integrates 'economic', ecological and ethical considerations. Ecological economics represents a new and essential development, but it still has much progress to make. In the meantime, environmental economics poses a threat to the health of the living world.

The objective of environmental economics is to incorporate environmental issues into the traditional framework of economics and thereby to make economics the formal decision-making system for problems that affect the environment. The agenda is to develop numerical methods that allow traditional economic effects and environmental effects to become mutually commensurable. This can be done either by providing government decision makers with methods of monetary measurement of environmental effects so that they can be added to monetary measures of traditional goods and services, or by creating private markets for 'environmental goods' so that free markets put prices on the environment just as they put prices on ordinary goods. Markets are supposed to carry out commensuration because they allow consumers to express their 'preferences' for environmental goods on a par with other goods. In this way, the effects of economic activity on the natural environment can be brought into the economist's optimising framework by making everything comparable using a single measure of value, the dollar.

The theoretical rationale for environmental economics is the 'total value framework'. Within the total value framework, all impacts of an activity or proposed activity can be thought of in terms of a single value measure so that decisions can be made by adding up the total values associated with different courses of action and selecting the course which generates the highest value. As we have seen, this is considered possible because the act of choice by humans implies that relative valuations are applied to all things, including 'non-marketed' goods like clean air, national parks and unpolluted rivers. So as people make choices that affect the environment they are *implicitly* applying economic values to the environment. This is a profound mistake; it represents the fatal flaw not just of environmental economics but of economics itself. It is, moreover, the fundamental but ill-formed criticism that ordinary people have of the influence of economics on public and private life. It is the reason why economists are often described facetiously as people who know the price of everything and the value of nothing. We will explore the implications and errors of the total value framework.

THE TOTAL VALUE FRAMEWORK

At the outset, the natural environment is defined as a 'resource' with all of the philosophical baggage that the notion carries with it. In the words of one of the standard texts:

> In economics the environment is viewed as a composite asset that provides a variety of services. It is a very special asset, to be sure, since it provides the life-support systems that sustain our very existence, but it is an asset nonetheless. *As with other assets*, we wish to prevent undue depreciation of the value of this asset so it may continue to provide us with aesthetic and life-sustaining services.[1]

'For as long as we place a high enough price on them', we might add. Economists approach the question of resource management by asking the question: how can the benefits to society be maximised by choosing among alternative uses? They argue that in most circumstances the allocation of resources to maximise social welfare is best left to private markets in which people's preferences for different goods are reflected in market prices. However, it is acknowledged that while this approach is valid for 'private goods' there is a whole class of 'public goods', including environmental ones, for which private markets are inadequate or non-existent. Public goods are goods which cannot be withheld from one person without withholding them from everyone. Examples include national defence, street lighting and clean air.

In addition, production of private goods can give rise to costs that are not borne by the private producer. Examples of these so-called externalities are the noise generated by factory machinery, extinction of species due to logging and the increased nutrient loads in streams from the application of fertilisers to agricultural land.

Where private markets have been inadequate for determining the correct quantities supplied and 'prices' of goods, economists have traditionally turned to the framework provided by cost-benefit analysis which in its extended form is the total value framework put into practice. Cost-benefit analysis is simply a tool of public policy used by governments to decide how to allocate public funds or whether to approve a private investment proposal that has significant social or environmental impacts.

As we saw, cost-benefit analysis is the traditional framework for answering the question of how to maximise social welfare, whether it be asked of a proposed office block, a new factory or an untouched native forest. It has three essential stages:

> the *identification* of all of the flows of tangible and intangible costs and benefits that will result from a proposed development or resource use;

> the placing of values or *prices* on each of these costs and benefits; and

> the *aggregation* of flows of money values with the application of a discount factor which attaches lower values to costs and benefits in the future than to current costs and benefits.

The difficult steps are the second stage—putting correct prices on the various effects—and the third stage—deciding on an appropriate discount rate for costs and benefits that occur in the future. These are discussed in turn.

The essential premiss of cost-benefit analysis is that choices must be made between competing uses of a resource; by making choices we explicitly or implicitly place valuations on the outcomes of alternative uses. Put starkly, if the decision is whether to log a forest or not, the essential question is whether the value of the timber is greater than the ecological values that would be destroyed.

To do such a cost-benefit analysis we need to have a correct price for the timber and a correct 'price' for the ecological effects such as loss of wildlife. The relative prices should reflect 'society's' relative valuations of, or preferences for, these two 'goods'. Arriving at the correct price of timber is quite easy because there are private markets for timber. However, economists recognise that market prices themselves may be misleading because markets are not 'perfect'. The value to society of wood production may not be reflected in figures reported in company accounts or official statistics. If that is the case, the prices need to be adjusted before being fed into the decision analysis. Under what circumstances are market prices misleading?

In economic theory, market prices reflect the true value to society of goods only under some strong assumptions. These assumptions are summarised in the term 'perfect competition'.

In practice, markets are often not perfect. Taxes and subsidies (such as the provision of forest roads to loggers free of charge) may result in market prices that overstate or understate the true value of using forests for wood production. In addition, monopoly prices (where there is only one seller in the market) reflect market power rather than economic efficiency. State forest services, for example, may set royalties on grounds other than maximisation of returns to society from publicly owned forest lands. Within the economic framework, price distortions caused by imperfect markets can lead to over-exploitation or under-use of a resource relative to society's preferences.

Techniques generally referred to as 'shadow pricing' are used to adjust market prices to obtain 'true' prices. These adjustments highlight the crucial distinction between private profitability and 'social' profitability, a distinction often not recognised by critics of economic approaches. A project or resource use that is very profitable for the private firms involved may make losses from a social viewpoint and, economists should argue, ought not to proceed.

This idea is illustrated by the example of stumpages paid to state forest services by timber companies for logs. The true stumpage could arguably include both the full costs incurred by the state forest services of providing the timber, a component reflecting the damage done to the ecosystem and perhaps a component reflecting the need for the state forest service to invest in regenerating forests for the future. Failure to account fully for these costs would result in the subsidisation of logging by the taxpayer and by those who value forests for their ecological qualities. Subsidies are generally considered to be inefficient from an economic point of view because they cause investment capital to be shifted out of more efficient industries and into less efficient industries. However, subsidies may be justified if there are social objectives from the use of a resource in addition to the objective of strict market efficiency. If full social-cost pricing means that commercial logging cannot be sustained then this may indicate that the forest's value in an alternative use, such as fauna preservation, may be higher.

Our simple example of cost-benefit analysis of a forest indicates that the economic approach can provide answers only if a 'price' can be put on the 'environmental goods' supplied by the forest. However, in practice it may not be necessary to quantify the environmental effects of a proposal since the returns to society on more traditional 'economic' grounds may turn out to be negative, even if the proposal would be privately profitable. This occurred in a dam project in the USA—the Tellico Dam project on the Little Tennessee River. This case is of particular significance as the dam site was (at the time of the analysis) thought to be the critical habitat of the snail darter fish (*Percina tanasi*). Careful economic analysis of the project by independent economists—analysis which specifically excluded quantification of ecological values (especially the survival of the snail darter)—showed that the project would have had net costs to the community. This was because the flooding of the area in question would have caused major damage to the recreation and tourist industries and because the price of hydro-electric power used to justify the investment was shown to be exaggerated. The analysis showed that, as is often the case, the returns to *society* from a development are lower than those to the private developer.

If the proposed dam had had net social *benefits* as a power-generating facility despite the damage to recreational amenities, it would have been necessary to attempt to estimate the 'value' of preservation of the snail darter. If preservation of the snail darter were shown to be sufficiently valuable to society, then the dam should not have proceeded. But how do we put a 'price' on a snail darter or, to return to our example, a pristine forest? Economists have developed several techniques in recent years which attempt to answer this question. Quite apart from the philosophical objections to 'putting a price on the environment', objections that will be raised soon, there are serious practical difficulties.

Before elaborating on these methods of pricing the environment, it is worth saying a few more words about the use of discount rates in cost-benefit analysis—the key to the third stage of the process mentioned above. As we saw, a discount rate is the obverse of an interest rate. Discounting means that benefits that accrue in the future are considered to be less valuable than the equivalent benefits consumed now. Economists use several arguments to justify discounting. People prefer a dollar now rather than a dollar in five years time firstly because there is uncertainty about the future (we might be dead), secondly because we expect to be better off in the future and extra dollars bestow diminishing 'utility' as our income rises, and thirdly because a dollar now can be put to productive use (not least by earning interest in a bank).

The use of discounting when environmental effects are involved raises serious difficulties. Is a koala to be considered less valuable in ten years time than it is now? How are we to deal with irreversible effects, such as the loss of an irreplaceable wilderness or a hole in the ozone layer? Are these to be considered less important because much of their impact is in the future? Uncertainty about the future suggests that irreversible effects be given special importance. The question of irreversible effects is also bound up with the 'option value' of resources in the future, a concept discussed in the next section. Clearly, the act of discounting presupposes the archetypal economic situation in which continuously reproducible goods are consumed for the purpose of maximising personal utility.

High discount rates mean that investments with long-term pay-offs or with effects that are uncertain are less likely to appear worthwhile. High discount rates also tend to encourage more rapid depletion of non-renewable resources. On the other hand, low discount rates in principle tend to lead to more developments overall and thus to a greater demand for natural resources. In practice, however, discount rates are used by governments to decide which projects should receive funding from a limited budget. If low discount rates lead to 'too many' projects appearing to be profitable then some other criterion, in addition to the economist's rate of return or net present value, will be needed to choose between projects. In fact, this often happens in an informal way. Additional criteria may include unquantifiable social goals such as regional equity, ecological goals such as species preservation, ethical goals such as the extension of native land rights, and old-fashioned political expediency.

It is not a question, then, of which discount rate is appropriate for the environment. Discounting is simply inappropriate for activities or developments that involve a significant environmental component. Unlike the commodities of traditional economics, which people prefer now rather than in the future, the environment cannot be thought of as a commodity for which there is a money value. People do not value the environment less in the future than they do now; quite the reverse (which would imply a negative discount rate). This only serves to drive home the fundamental point: economic goods and the environment cannot be reduced to a common measure, neither dollars nor anything else, and thereby added together. The decision-making process is not appropriately one of private market valuations but of social and political decisions in which the advantages and disadvantages of a course of action are weighed up informally. In this way, all aspects of an issue can be brought into the process—the economic values, the ecological values and the social values, all mixed in with the ethical and political implications of each decision.

THE DOLLAR VALUE OF A KOALA

Economists see the natural environment as a collection of resources which have several competing, and sometimes complementary, uses. Each of these uses has a value which may be expressed in dollars or some other *numéraire*. Although it may be very difficult to determine in practice the dollar values of environmental effects, nevertheless, economists argue, we 'in effect' place relative valuations on the environment because we make choices between environmental and ordinary goods. Of course this implies a wholly instrumentalist way of viewing the world since it assumes that something has value only if it is useful to humans. The instrumentalist bias is something fundamental to Western society, not only to economics, and we will return to this objection. The instrumentalist view by definition excludes moral and ethical considerations from personal and social decisions, because the purpose of the economic calculus is to discover what is the 'right' course of action. The right course of action is the one that maximises the utility or welfare of those affected.

It is apparent that the instrumentalist philosophy in itself implies an economic definition of value, and this in turn means that values can in principle be measured in monetary terms. The political correlate of this view of the world is often referred to as 'libertarianism' or 'economic rationalism'. It differs from old-fashioned conservatism in that the latter asserts that moral values matter and is unafraid to advocate positions based on moral stances rather than economic calculations. Economic rationalists, on the other hand, believe that unfettered markets, which they maintain are value-neutral, will generate the best decisions because they do no more than allow the free expression of people's preferences (which may or may not reflect personal moral views). In reality, the economic rationalists are just as much influenced by their own moral positions as anyone else; they differ in that they are unaware of it.

In order to incorporate 'environmental goods' into the total value framework it has been first necessary for environmental economics to define more precisely what the 'values' of these goods are. Environmental economics sees resources as having a range of different values corresponding to the ways that the resource can be used by people. What are the main types of values of resources? Environmental economists generally divide them into two types, use values and non-use values.

Use values Traditionally, the focus of economics has been almost exclusively on the direct utility (i.e. usefulness) obtained from consumption of goods bought and sold in markets. The use values of forests, for example, include timber values as well as other commercial uses of forests such as mining, bee-keeping and seed-collection.

In more recent times, economists have identified some less tangible and less direct values that can be obtained from the use of resources. Most obviously, a natural area may have recreational value. In the anthropocentric view of the economists, some animals are said to provide recreational value because people like to look at them in zoos or catch sight of them in the wild. This is another consumptive value in the sense that people can go to a zoo or a national park and 'consume' the recreational properties of the park. This is known as a 'user benefit'.

Non-use values In addition it is acknowledged by environmental economics that there may be various non-user benefits. These accrue to individuals from the preservation of environmental resources even though the individuals do not directly 'consume' the resources. These sorts of values try to capture the public's and the ecologist's perception of the more diffuse and intangible values of the environment. What are these? In the new terminology, the principal non-use values are referred to as existence value, option value and bequest value.

Existence value is the benefit obtained by people simply from the knowledge that a 'resource' exists. For example, the fact that spotted-tailed quolls exist gives them value, even though one may never see them. Their existence somehow makes people 'feel good'. This is a stark example of the way in which economics can transform a complex and subtle human sentiment into a commodity to be bought and sold.

Option value is the benefit enjoyed by retaining the option to use an environmental resource in the future. People may choose not to deplete an environmental asset now but to preserve it in order that they will have the option to deplete it or preserve it in the future. In addition, there are many uncertainties surrounding the management of any ecosystem and, as a general rule, the risks of irreversible damage increase with the degree of human intervention. Ecologists often highlight the lack of factual information needed for the effective management of renewable and non-renewable resources exposed to significant human intervention. In addition, many people attach value to delay so that decisions are held off until more information becomes available. The decision to preserve is interpreted by economists as an expression of a willingness to pay an insurance premium measured by the user benefits that are foregone for a period.

Moreover, as time proceeds, preferences may change. There may be benefit in delaying decisions to develop an area in the expectation that society's valuation of 'environmental goods', such as unspoiled wilderness, grows relative to that of the usual commercial products.

Bequest value is the benefit the current generation is thought to obtain by preserving the environment for use by future generations. This is a sort of inter-generational option value. The benefits of preservation accrue to our descendants rather than to ourselves. For example, one of the benefits accruing to us from the preservation of an endangered species is the good feeling that we obtain from knowing that our children will be able to see it (or, indeed, to obtain existence, option and bequest values from it themselves).

These values cannot be determined by way of market prices that express consumers' preferences because markets do not exist. Nevertheless, a 'demand' for them appears to exist because people express their preferences through 'non-market' mechanisms such as the political process. Politicians respond to consumers' demands for preservation. The development of the concepts of user and non-user benefits illustrates graphically how economics can take what are essentially social and political decisions and squash them into the utilitarian framework provided by 'rational economic man' so that the market can render redundant political and community decision making.

Non-use values and some types of use values are known as non-market values because private markets do not exist for them. In order to incorporate all values into the total value framework, non-market values must somehow be measured in the same units as market values, that is, dollars. Environmental economists have developed a number of techniques for assessing non-market values. These techniques rely either on information from real markets for other goods that are related to the 'good' in question, or they rely on the construction of 'hypothetical markets' to generate the required information.

Among the related-market approaches are the travel cost method and the hedonic pricing technique. The travel cost method infers the value of, say, the recreational benefits of a national park from actual expenditure by tourists on travel to and from the park. The more people are willing to pay to get to the park the greater the apparent recreational benefits that can be obtained.

The hedonic pricing technique is usually used to measure the value of an environmental good by assessing the impact on property prices of some change in the environmental good. For example, statistical analysis of the factors that determine house prices around an airport can tell us how much the value of houses is influenced by aircraft noise. Other things being equal (the purpose of the statistical analysis), lower purchase prices for houses affected by noise pollution reflect the amount of 'compensation' that people are willing to accept for tolerating the noise. This method has also been used to assess the impact of land degradation on rural property prices.

A more commonly used related-market method is the damage cost method. The value of environmental degradation is measured by the cost of rectifying the damage done to it. For instance, water pollution caused by a chemical factory is valued at the cost of cleaning up the river by installing pollution abatement equipment at the factory. As another example, the costs of climate change due to global warming can be measured by the costs of building dykes to keep back rising sea waters and the costs of moving populations from affected areas. Extraordinary as this may seem, there have been several analyses by respected economists that have done precisely this. We will comment later on how these measures ignore the complexity and uncertainty of changes to ecological processes by focussing on the short-term economic costs of environmental degradation.

The contingent valuation method of valuing environmental goods constructs a hypothetical market for the good in question. It is used in particular for assessing non-use values of the environment such as existence value. Individuals are asked how much they would be willing to pay to preserve some aspect of the environment, or how much compensation they would be willing to accept to offset the loss of some environmental attribute. Essentially, the contingent valuation method creates an imaginary market for an 'environmental good' by means of a public opinion survey. The good in question is described to the respondents who are then asked how much they would be willing to pay to 'buy' the environmental amenity. The 'good' might be an animal population threatened by a housing development, a park free of logging or a river without pollution. The theory is that by creating a market situation, respondents become consumers who are compelled to make a trade-off between their desire for environmental preservation and their desire for the ordinary goods on which they would otherwise spend their money.

The valuation of non-marketed environmental 'goods' is a rapidly growing field particularly in the USA where contingent valuation is now a legislative requirement in assessing the impacts of water resource developments. Governments are turning to the method in order to try to balance the commercial benefits and costs of a development against the environmental costs and benefits which are not reflected in markets and prices. Contingent valuation surveys are recognised in courts of law in the USA in assessing damages to the environment. Exxon paid out over $1 billion in compensation for the Exxon-Valdez oil spill disaster, often referred to as the USA's worst ever environmental disaster. The pay-out was made after contingent valuation surveys seemed likely to show a huge public demand for compensation. Exxon had hired more than one Nobel Prize winning economist in an attempt to discredit the technique. US courts have upheld its validity.

A contingent valuation survey to estimate the value of endangered whooping cranes in the USA was carried out by Stoll and Johnson.[2] They surveyed visitors to the Aransas National Wildlife Refuge in Texas to measure recreation, option and existence values. They also conducted a mail survey of residents of Texas, Chicago, New York, Atlanta and Los Angeles to measure the existence and option values of the cranes. Stoll and Johnson found that visitors to Aransas National Wildlife Refuge were willing to pay about $17 per year in order to preserve the option of seeing the whooping cranes in the future, while Texas residents were willing to pay $10 per year. Out-of-state residents were willing to pay $13 per year. The existence values per household for visitors to the refuge averaged $9 a year, and a little over $1 per year for Texas and out-of-state residents. As existence and option values of an endangered species such as the whooping crane can be enjoyed simultaneously by all households in the US (and the world for that matter) Stoll and Johnson's aggregate estimate of the United States' option and existence values for whooping cranes was $573 million annually, a large amount of money.

In order to estimate option, existence, bequest and recreational values of water quality, one analysis used the viability of fish populations, one of the key characteristics of good water quality, in a contingent valuation study.[3] They found values of $56 per household for recreation use and $22 per household for option value. The existence value (defined as clean water serving as the natural habitat of plants, fish and wildlife, even if respondents knew for certain they would not use the river for water-based recreation) was found to be $25 per non-user household and $34 per user household. Values of $17 per non-user household and $33 per user household were reported for bequest value.

In Australia, a government-sponsored national contingent valuation survey was conducted in 1990 to assess the preservation benefits of an area within Kakadu National Park that would have been disturbed by a proposed gold mine. It was found that Australians collectively would be willing to pay at least A$640 million per year to preserve the area, a sum that greatly exceeded the projected A$82 million total profit from gold mining.[4]

The values uncovered by contingent valuation surveys tend to be 'high', higher than might be expected, and often high enough to permit the benefits of preserving the natural environment to outweigh the benefits of exploiting it for commercial gain. This has led to the peculiar situation in which business people and economists who work for them vigorously oppose the use of the technique even though they are ideologically predisposed to accept the application of hard-nosed economic techniques. Conservationists, on the other hand, are very suspicious of any attempt to place dollar values on the environment but often find that the results of applications of the technique support their case. Thus business favours the technique but rejects the results, while conservationists reject the technique but favour the results.

THE ERROR OF NON-MARKET VALUATION

The contingent valuation method in particular has attracted a great deal of attention in recent years. It will serve as an excellent vehicle for developing a critique of non-market valuation, the total value framework and environmental economics itself.

There are several practical difficulties with the contingent valuation method that are acknowledged by practitioners. These include strategic bias, accurate definition of the 'good', and hypothetical bias. Strategic bias arises when respondents try to influence the overall outcome of the survey by exaggerating or understating their true willingness to pay for the environmental good because they know that in practice they will not have to pay. The exaggeration of one's actual willingness to pay is akin to the free-rider problem. The problem of strategic bias can be largely overcome by the use of face-to-face interviewing and the 'referendum model'. In the latter model, respondents are asked if they would pay a specified amount, to which they may only respond 'yes' or 'no'. A carefully designed survey strategy can by these methods minimise the risk that strategic behaviour will influence the results of the survey.

Successful creation of a hypothetical market for an environmental good demands that it must be possible to define the 'good' very clearly so that respondents understand without ambiguity what they are 'buying'. This requirement rules out the use of the contingent valuation method for putting prices on many environmental amenities. For example, the issue of the greenhouse effect is so complex that it would not lend itself sensibly to a willingness-to-pay survey. The amounts that respondents say they are willing to pay depend heavily on the selection of information that is presented to them. Thus protagonists will often claim that the information given to respondents was biased so that the valuations uncovered by the survey are inaccurate.

Hypothetical bias refers to the effect of respondents failing to give serious, considered answers to survey questions because the situation is too hypothetical. It arises when the survey does not set up a believable situation in which respondents might be required to pay. This often rules out the use of contingent valuation. The extent of this problem depends very much on the institutional context of the survey. If a local government asks local residents by how much they would be willing to see their land rates rise in order to fund a new wildlife sanctuary, the survey has credibility because the local government could very easily raise land rates for such a purpose.

Many of these problems are well recognised and can be minimised, or at least have their impacts described, by good survey design and survey method.[5] One of the more serious limitations of all non-market valuation methods is that they can generally provide no more than an estimate at a single point in time of the 'price' of the environmental good. For planning purposes, however, decision makers need to have an idea of how valuations will change over time. This is possible for ordinary goods for which there might be futures markets or good commercial forecasts. In addition, changing prices are much less of a problem in the case of ordinary goods because there are usually several actual or potential substitutes for them. If their prices rise in the future other goods can be substituted for them. The physical supply of environmental attributes generally cannot be increased. As their supply diminishes due to exploitation, their importance to people increases. In addition, social attitudes are shifting in favour of preservation so that people are increasingly willing to sacrifice more of other things to save the natural environment.

The value people attach to the environment arises from two basic sources:

> the real economic costs of environmental degradation such as the impact of land degradation on agricultural productivity, the costs of providing safe and palatable drinking water, and the health costs of air pollution; and

> the aesthetic or ethical concerns that people have about environmental degradation arising from the feeling that the natural environment—its landscapes, its flora and its wildlife—has been exploited too hard and for too long.

The first set of concerns appears more 'hard-headed', but there is nothing invalid about the second set. The latter concerns are prone to rapid change as social attitudes shift. The greening of community attitudes in the West in the last decade or so would have been difficult to predict. How can we know what they will be in another ten years? Yet if the total value framework of environmental economics is to provide the answers to our environmental problems, these future values must be known. Unfortunately, environmental economics cannot provide the answers.

The more serious difficulties with non-market valuation of the natural environment are philosophical and go to the core of the economic approach to the world. These will be elaborated on presently. It ought to be noted, however, that the advocates of non-market valuation are unquestionably the more liberal members of the economics profession. There is another school of 'environmental economists' which views non-market valuation with suspicion and even derision because it presupposes a major role for governments in making decisions. This other school, known as free market environmentalism, argues that environmental problems arise because the government is too involved and that it should be left to the private activities of individuals in the marketplace to express their preferences for environmental preservation. This line of argument is much more consistent with the theory of the economics textbooks, and has gained considerable influence in recent years. It is therefore worthy of examination.

FREE MARKET ENVIRONMENTALISM

Free market environmentalism focusses on the issue of ownership or property rights over resources. The property rights approach argues that the natural environment has been degraded because it does not belong to anyone. It is therefore treated as a 'free good' which people feel they can use up or dump their pollution into without damage to themselves. It is argued that if forests, rivers and even the atmosphere were privately owned the owners would have an incentive to protect them. In effect, then, the property rights approach advocates that public goods be turned into private goods through the granting of private property rights. Private markets in which environmental goods are traded alongside ordinary goods will then ensure that the environment is protected to the extent that private consumers want to protect it.

In contrast to the interventionist foundations of cost-benefit analysis—which accepts a significant role for government—the property rights approach is associated with economists who strongly emphasise market-based, and thus private, decision making. The appeal of free market environmentalism to many in the economics profession is that it makes redundant the detailed investigation of the costs and benefits of government decision making. The information required for optimal decisions is contained in the supply prices and the demand prices of resource owners and resource buyers in the market. Market signals replace government and community deliberation. This fits very comfortably with the ideological predisposition of modern neoclassical economics to oppose a role for government except in cases of absolutely unavoidable market failure.

The property rights approach requires the creation of markets for goods that are not presently exchanged in markets, such as state-owned forests, national parks, clean air, unpolluted rivers and endangered species. These markets would be established by governments defining legal frameworks where the ownership or rights to the use of a resource are vested in individuals, companies or groups. By auctioning property rights to individuals or private corporations, people will be able to give effect to their preferences for environmental preservation by buying and selling the rights to use the resources in question. It is argued that many 'environmental goods' such as the preservation of wildlife or genetic diversity are under-supplied because the lack of property rights to these resources limits the net return entrepreneurs can obtain from their use.

Free market environmentalists argue that once property rights over resources have been clearly defined and enforced, including the rules for transfer of these rights through sale in the marketplace, then the cause of conflict between economists and ecologists will disappear. The demands for competing uses of natural resources, such as the timber values versus the preservation values of forests, would find full expression in well-defined markets for the goods in question. If conservationists value preservation of an area sufficiently highly then they will individually or collectively buy the rights to the area and use it as their preferences dictate. As long as the relevant markets are competitive so that the prices reflect 'true' values, entrepreneurs have an incentive to manage resources to provide whatever individuals value. When property rights are well-defined, secure, enforceable and transferable then the owners of those resources take good care of them. Their future market value may depend on conservation of the qualities of the resources that some people find desirable.

Most people view this set of ideas as a wild economists' fantasy. There are several obvious problems with the property rights approach. It is difficult to envisage how in practice the allocation of property rights for environmental goods such as visual beauty, clean air and maintenance of ecosystem processes would occur. For example, it is possible to imagine an entrepreneur charging visitors to see the last remaining representatives of a species of forest fauna such as Javan rhinos or spotted owls. However, this situation is an unusual one for the vast majority of fauna which are not reduced to remnant populations and which are likely to be geographically dispersed or difficult to observe. In addition, the entrepreneur could not capture the 'non-use values' (such as existence and bequest values) enjoyed by society, values which may form the greatest part of the total value of the species in question. Whales are a good case. Most 'public goods' simply cannot be privatised without losing some of their essential qualities.

It would be quite feasible under the free market scheme for whalers to pay the highest price for 'rights' over whales and to hunt them to extinction. That would simply reflect the relative monetary valuations of whale eaters versus conservationists. There is no room for the ethics of species preservation, or for the inequality of purchasing power or for the primacy of community decision making in situations where it is demanded. The entire process of exploiting or preserving the natural environment is left to the vagaries of today's market in which private individuals in the pursuit of their self-interest weigh up the dollar values of ozone depletion, global warming and biodiversity against the dollar value of a plastic bag full of groceries.

It is sometimes acknowledged by free market environmentalists that the allocation of property rights (over a forest, for instance) needs to be accompanied by specified obligations which circumscribe the uses to which the property may be put (for example, rules which govern logging practices). These are necessary, it is conceded, to protect the public goods component of the resource that cannot be sold by the owner (for example, the existence value of a forest). In practice, privatisation would require in each case a complex list of interlocking rights and obligations for every party that is in some way affected by any use of the resource in question. Quite apart from the problems of actually defining and then allocating the rights and obligations, serious practical difficulties arise in trying to monitor whether the obligations are being adhered to.

In addition, the property rights solution may result in insufficient attention being paid to the needs of future generations which cannot participate in the current market. The private owner may have an incentive to maintain the quality of the good in question but the entrepreneur cannot rely on future, as yet unspent, income to meet costs today. One of the favourite solutions of economists to the critical problem of tropical deforestation is to grant long leases over forests to logging companies. Long leases, it is argued, will encourage sustained yield logging and it will not be in the interests of logging companies to allow deforestation. It seems to other people, people less prone to leap instinctively to market solutions, that it would be folly indeed to pin our hopes of stopping massive deforestation on the theory that business people will adopt a commercial time horizon of 50-100 years if only given the opportunity. It may make perfect business sense to completely denude the forests and then to move the accumulated profits into some other enterprise, perhaps real estate speculation or a Coca-Cola franchise. Moreover, there is always a tendency when times are hard for private individuals to 'eat their capital', bringing about an irreversible loss. All of this bespeaks the natural desirability of investing ownership and care of environmental assets in communities and representative governments.

This suggests two reasons why leaving environmental preservation wholly to private markets is a misguided and dangerous solution. The first reason relates to both efficiency and distributional considerations. The horn of a rhinoceros has value to many people when it is on the end of a rhino's nose. Many people derive positive feelings from the knowledge that rhinos roam free, 'cornu intacticus' so to speak, and may be willing to pay to preserve it that way. On the other hand, ground rhino horn is extremely valuable as an aphrodisiac. However, a horn ground up as an aphrodisiac benefits only the person who swallows it and conceivably one or two other persons who may experience the effects of the user's heightened ardour. In the latter case, the price of the rhino horn, which is now a private good, is determined, according to the economics textbooks, by the marginal valuation of the person purchasing it as an aphrodisiac. This value is very high and has led to black rhinos being poached to the point of extinction. When attached to free-roaming rhinos, the value of the horn is determined by the sum of the valuations of all of the people who value the free-roaming rhinos. In that case, consumption by one person does not exclude consumption by others. Even though the consumer of aphrodisiacs may place a very high price on the rhino horn, it is almost certainly more efficient from a social viewpoint (not to mention the rhino's) to leave it where it is. Equity considerations may strengthen the case for forbidding the privatisation of the horn if consumers of aphrodisiacs are richer than lovers of free-roaming rhinos.

This is all consistent with economic theory. The free-market environmentalists want a market to be created for rhinos in which conservationists could buy the rhinos and preserve them. But it is illegal now to kill rhinos; the poachers are not likely to have greater respect for private ownership than public ownership. Moreover, conservationists may well argue that, to the extent that conservationists represent the sentiments of the public, they already own the rhinos and should not be required to buy them.

The second reason supporting the role of communities and government in the protection of the natural environment goes to the heart of the way that economics constructs the world. There is considerable evidence that people think about 'public goods' such as environmental amenities in a way quite different to the way they think about private goods.[6] In the former case, people operate in a public-spirited mode in which the interests of others, including future generations, play a more prominent role. When we play a part in a community decision we like to think of ourselves as responsible citizens. We tend to ask ourselves what is good for our community or our country rather than what is in our personal best interests. In the latter case, private market behaviour tends to be much more individualistic and self-centred. Our boundaries of concern do not extend beyond ourselves and our families. In other words, when we are in the ballot box we do not think and behave in the same way that we do in the supermarket. This is one of the principal problems with contingent valuation surveys: they ask respondents to put a supermarket price on something respondents value socially. The *qualities* of social and private valuations differ. To the extent that social and private valuations are commensurable, their quantities may also be different if people are asked to determine valuations in more social settings such as a discussion group, a public submission or a ballot box. Thus, in circumstances where a 'resource' has a significant 'public good' component, it is appropriate for decisions about its use to be made by community mechanisms rather than private markets.

There are good reasons then for believing that many commonly held resources are properly owned by the community or by representative governments. In general, the case for public ownership of natural assets becomes stronger as the 'public' component of the goods increases. It is a myth that environmental degradation has occurred because no one owns the resources which are being polluted or disturbed. In reality, environmental degradation is not due to inadequately defined private property rights but rather to the inadequately enforced rights of the public to community-owned property. The tragedy of the commons argument is wrong in so far as it attributes the results of bad management and inadequate enforcement to the incorrect allocation of property rights.

The oft-stated belief that many environmental goods are not owned by anyone appears contrary to the view, held by many in the community, that these goods are in fact owned by the community. As the forests are progressively destroyed, whether in Borneo, Oregon or South-East Australia, communities increasingly assert their 'rights of ownership' over the environmental attributes of the forests that they fear will be lost or degraded. Moreover, as community values change so do perceptions of property rights. Aboriginal land rights in Australia are another case in point; politicians twenty or thirty years ago would have found it unthinkable to grant title to huge tracts of land to traditional owners. In a sense, then, the property rights have already been allocated and they are held collectively. The moral question is not how much people should pay for access to these resources but whether entrepreneurs can be induced to pay enough to the community for the community to relinquish ownership or rights to exploitation. Just as the community may decide to sell mining rights to a mining company, the community may decide that the environmental losses due to mining outweigh any amount a mining company may be willing to pay. For a government newly convinced by the free market environmentalist argument, such public attitudes create difficulties when it attempts to sell off community property rights to the environment.

FUNDAMENTAL PROBLEMS WITH ENVIRONMENTAL ECONOMICS

The fundamental problem with environmental economics is that it allows us to be only one thing, private economic agents. This creature, *homo economicus*, is merely one aspect of human behaviour, one that has emerged as a distinct concept in Western societies only in the last two or three centuries. It is an aspect, moreover, that many thoughtful people regard as venal, exploitative and self-destructive. To hold it up as the ideal against which all must be judged and on which all decisions should be based appears to many to be ideological folly of the first order. Therein lies the danger of the attempt by environmental economics to integrate environmental decisions into the framework provided by neoclassical economics. All of the criticisms of economics that are made elsewhere in this book apply to environmental economics. Indeed, the strength of the criticisms is redoubled in the case of environmental economics because environmental issues make it so obvious that the world is much more, and we as beings are much more, than economics allows.

Environmental economics defines the natural world as a list of commodities that can be in principle, and should be in practice, bought and sold in the marketplace. To do this it must first dissect the natural environment into its 'components', a dissection that is motivated by the mentality of exploitation and consumption by humans. The integrity of an ecosystem is a concept that does not fit into the reductionist analytical mind-set. In a system composed of self-centred, rational individuals, the unity of the creation can only be an inconvenience for efficient allocation. For environmental economics, the total value framework is a natural extension of the utilitarian 'ethic' in which the natural world, duly dissected into a catalogue of resources, has value solely because it is useful to humans and because humans are willing to pay for it in the marketplace. This means that humans have arrogated to themselves absolute rights over the natural world including the right to sell parts of the natural world to others. The notion that private ownership is everywhere the natural order imbues the whole discipline. But if we take the natural world to be an immanent part of all of us, as living within us as well as existing outside of us, then the alienation of the natural world is the alienation of ourselves from ourselves.

Decisions over human impacts on the natural environment are as much ethical decisions as economic ones; and the values in question are moral as well as monetary. Yet environmental economics—in setting out to make all things commensurable in terms of money—permits only *homo economicus*, the selfish calculator of the textbooks. In this view of the world, society is no more than the sum of its atomistic parts and social outcomes should emerge from the private decisions of individuals because individuals are truly 'free' only when they are expressing their personal preferences. There is an explicit belief within neoclassical economics that private is better because only private markets allow individuals without hindrance to express their preferences truly.

In the world of economic agents only those who pay have a vote, and those with more money have more votes because their preferences have greater impact on the market. This reflects the belief that those able to participate in markets have the right to determine the values of the world's resources. The interests of future generations and of life forms other than humans cannot find expression, except insofar as these other interests are proxied by the market behaviour of humans in the present. The world and its natural riches becomes a supermarket in which the biosphere is preserved and nurtured only to the extent permitted by the self-centred economist within. The environment is treated no differently from any commodity to be found on the shelves of the local supermarket. If we accept that the natural environment is no more than a collection of resources to be sold to the highest bidder then we cannot object to the programme of Gary Becker and his followers who want to transform marriage, child bearing, drug addiction and burglary into products of rational economic calculation. Nor could we demur when a well-functioning market drives an endangered species to extinction.

Some of these problems emerge with great clarity in contingent valuation surveys which attempt to put monetary values on environmental amenities by simulating markets for environmental goods. When respondents to these surveys are asked how much they would be willing to pay to protect a national park from mining or to have unpolluted air or to prevent an animal species from extinction, many refuse to answer. These people refuse to see the issue cast in economic terms, despite the pressure provided by the questionnaire itself, and maintain that it is an ethical issue that cannot be monetised, or a social issue that is the responsibility of the government and not a question of individual payments by private citizens. In other words, these respondents refuse to disavow what perhaps most respondents feel, that these are ethical and social issues that require ethical and social decisions, not economic ones. As a result, and to the great consternation of environmental economics, some citizens appear to place an 'infinite value' on some aspects of environmental preservation (a few people may even be willing to give their lives), and it takes but one such respondent to give an average price that is infinite. Rather than concede that the issue is not solely economic, and that the appropriate decision process is a social one, it becomes necessary to ignore these responses.

Environmental economics, then, is fundamentally in error because it accepts and reinforces *homo economicus* in a context where the private, self-centred individual is misplaced. Arising directly from the perspective of environmental economics is the belief that we have environmental problems because we have not carried out enough analysis, because we have not incorporated all of the information into our economic calculations through our market behaviour. We are not beset by environmental disaster because of the sort of people we are, or because of the type of society we have constructed; we are beset by environmental disaster because we have not been rational enough. The answer then is not a reconsideration of our priorities, or a reassertion of our ethical selves, or a transformation of society; the answer lies in making better calculations of how to increase our wealth. Instead of being a product of too much rational, self-interested calculation, our environmental calamity has become a product of not enough economics.

One of the most disturbing examples of the conceptual imperialism of environmental economics can be found in the debate over global warming. There is now a school of increasingly *blasé* economists who believe that the enhanced greenhouse effect due to industrial pollution may not be a bad thing. After all, the argument goes, while some parts of the world will be flooded and others will become intolerably hot, some regions will become wetter and this will improve agricultural productivity. A thorough assessment of the costs and benefits of global warming (including the benefits of improved agricultural productivity, the costs of building dykes, the costs of transmigration to avoid famine and so on) may well show that the benefits exceed the costs, especially when compared to the alternative scenario, *viz.* a dramatic reduction in dependence on fossil fuels. It would be entirely consistent with this line of argument to advocate measures to speed up global warming so that we can enjoy the benefits of a hotter planet sooner.

The most influential economist advocating this line of argument is William Nordhaus who in a string of papers has analysed the economic impact of the enhanced greenhouse effect on the USA.[7] Nordhaus begins with the most fundamental assumption of economics, that a course of action is desirable according to whether or not the sum of the economic benefits outweighs the sum of the economic costs.

> Whether preventive action should be taken depends on the costs of preventing GHG [greenhouse gas] emissions relative to the damages that the GHGs would cause if they continued unchecked.

Fortunately, Nordhaus reassures us,

> Most of the US economy has little <u>direct</u> interaction with climate, and the impacts of climate change are likely to be very small in these sectors. For example, cardiovascular surgery and microprocessor fabrication are undertaken in carefully controlled environments and are unlikely to be directly affected by climate change.

Nordhaus calculates that only three per cent of national output in the USA is produced in 'climate-sensitive sectors'—mainly agriculture—while another 10 per cent is generated by 'moderately impacted sectors', such as construction, water transportation and energy utilities.

However, it is by no means obvious that these sectors will be affected negatively. In agriculture, for instance, while rising temperatures may reduce yields, the fertilization effect of higher levels of carbon dioxide will tend to raise yields. As another example, 'investments in water skiing will appreciate while those in snow skiing will depreciate.'

When the money values of all of these effects are added up and suitably discounted Nordhaus comes to the soothing conclusion that US citizens at least have little to worry about.

> In sum, the economic impact upon the U.S. economy of the climatic changes induced by a doubling of CO_2 concentrations is likely to be small . . . around one-fourth of 1 percent of national income.

There are many responses to the simple-minded economists' view of the relationship between humans and the biosphere that underlies Nordhaus' analysis.[8] But one attitude stands out, and that is the belief that faced with a potentially drastic change to the entire global ecosystem we can add up the costs and benefits to humans and decide the extent to which we want to modify the Earth's atmosphere. The clear implication of the idea of an optimal level of greenhouse gas emissions is that economic rationality requires human beings to optimally transform the Earth's climate and any other aspect of the natural environment in order to maximise our welfare.

Nordhaus's conclusions have been influential in slowing down international action to tackle the greenhouse problem. His results show that any but the easiest actions to slow greenhouse warming would be too costly compared to the calculated small net costs of global warming in the longer term.

Nordhaus concedes that his analysis fails to take account of 'goods and services' that are difficult to value monetarily. If only he could do it in practice, Nordhaus would reduce the ecological and ethical effects of global warming to commodities to be bought and sold in the marketplace, for then, according to economic theory, they would be valued precisely according to their contribution to human welfare.

> Many valuable goods and services escape the net of the national income accounts and might affect the calculations [of the economic effects of climate change in the U.S.]. Among the areas of importance are human health, biological diversity, amenity values of everyday life and leisure, and environmental quality. Some people will place a high moral, aesthetic, or environmental value on preventing climate change, but I know of no serious estimates of what people are willing to pay to stop greenhouse warming.[9]

Even though Nordhaus admits that within his own framework there are important effects that are excluded, this does not prevent him from reaching the conclusion that global warming is not a very serious problem and that therefore policies to reduce carbon emissions substantially are unnecessary. Within his own framework of cost-benefit analysis, he attributes zero values to human health, biological diversity, amenity values of everyday life and leisure, and environmental quality—every effect other than those that the national accounts, and thus private markets, permit him to value monetarily. Given the use to which this sort of analysis is inevitably put by the fossil fuel lobby and governments swayed by it, Nordhaus' analysis can only be described as irresponsible; it pretends to draw conclusions based on scientific analysis when in fact they only express Nordhaus' personal opinions.

Although he feels the need to disavow such a conclusion, the inescapable logic of Nordhaus' method of analysis could just as easily lead to the conclusion that welfare could be maximised by increasing the rate at which greenhouse gases are pumped into the atmosphere so that humanity does not have to wait so long to enjoy the benefits of global warming. Indeed, Nordhaus finally admits that 'the greenhouse effect might on balance actually be economically advantageous'.

In the face of his conclusion that sharp reductions in carbon emissions would be too costly, Nordhaus considers some cheaper measures to reduce greenhouse gases, measures that reflect a faith in technological fixes that would have most engineers blushing. He is favourably disposed to 'climatic engineering solutions'—what he calls the global equivalent of turning on an air conditioner—schemes that include launching huge space mirrors to deflect solar radiation. One promising approach would be to

> create a sunscreen by sending tiny particulates into the stratosphere to cool the earth. These particles could be shot up with 16" naval rifles, lifted by hydrogen balloons, or deposited by tuning the engines of aircraft to burn somewhat richer than normal.

This statement may serve as the apotheosis of the brave new world of scientific determinism ushered in by the Enlightenment three centuries ago. If science and industry cause a problem, even one as overwhelmingly complex as global warming, then the answer is not to tackle the problem but to use more science and industry to counter the effects. That is true faith; its function is to replace respect for the Earth's mysteries with the arrogant certainty of the rational economic calculator.

This whole line of argument is breath-taking for its faith in humanity's ability to control the natural world. With global climate change, we are talking about change to a complete system of unimaginable complexity; a system whose intricacies we have barely begun to understand. Who can possibly predict the consequences of global warming except at the crudest level? And what does it reflect about our respect for Gaia to imagine that we can regulate the whole to suit our own needs? The belief that twentieth-century humans can manipulate a global ecosystem that has evolved to its present delicate equilibrium over millions of years is perhaps the lowest point of the contempt for Nature that has so characterised the scientific vision of the last three centuries, a vision to which most economists still naively cling.

1   Tom Tietenberg, *Environmental and Natural Resource Economics*, Second Edition (Scott, Foresman and Co., Glenview, Illinois, 1988), my emphasis

2   Stoll, J. & Johnson, L., 'Concepts of value, nonmarket valuation and the case of the Whooping Crane' (Wildlife Management Institute, Washington DC, 1984)

3   Walsh, R. *et al.*, 'Option values, preservation values and recreational benefits of improved water quality: A case study of the South Platte River basin, Colorado' (Environmental Protection Agency, Washington DC, 1978)

4   Imber, D., Wilks, L. & Stevenson, G., *A Contingent Valuation Survey of the Kakadu Conservation Zone* (Resource Assessment Commission, Australian Government Publishing Service, Canberra, 1990)

5   See the bible of contingent valuation by Robert Mitchell and Richard Carson, *Using Surveys to Value Public Goods: The Contingent Valuation Method* (Resources for the Future, Washington DC, 1989)

6   See, for instance, Amartya Sen, *Resources, Values and Development* (Harvard University Press, Cambridge, Mass., 1984)

7   In particular, see William Nordhaus, 'Economic Approaches to Greenhouse Warming' (Yale University, 1990) and 'To Slow or Not To Slow: The Economics of the Greenhouse Effect' (Yale University 1990), from which the quotations below are taken.

8   See in particular G. Daily, P. Ehrlich, H. Mooney and A. Ehrlich, 'Greenhouse economics: Learn before you leap', *Ecological Economics*, Vol. 4, No. 1, October 1991. These authors take up Nordhaus' argument that the best guess of an increase of 1.5 degrees C to 4.5 degrees C in the Earth's temperature is trivial because most people experience greater temperature fluctuations daily. 'At the peak of the last ice age, the mean surface temperature of the Earth was 'only' 5 degrees C cooler than it is now. But then, an ice cap a mile or more thick covered most of Canada and parts of both Eurasia and northern United Sates (including all of Manhattan)'. (p. 3)

9   He even goes so far as to concede that 'many values cannot be incorporated into a quantitative cost-benefit analysis. . . . While being unable to put a price tag on Venice, we might decide that it is unacceptable to take actions that threaten Venice's existence'.

4   THE PRICE OF GOD AT CORONATION HILL

THE BULA LEGEND

Coronation Hill is located in the hinterland of Kakadu National Park in Northern Australia. It lies close to the South Alligator River in the traditional lands of the Jawoyn Aborigines. Coronation Hill is known to the Jawoyn (pronounced 'jar-won') as Guratba. Guratba is sacred and is registered in the Northern Territory as a sacred site. It lies in an area known to the Jawoyn as the Sickness Country. The Jawoyn have inhabited the area for tens of thousands of years and it is rich in archaeological sites. In common with other Aboriginal tribes, the Jawoyn have a creation myth. It centres on the figure of Bula.

A full account of the Bula tradition is not possible because significant parts of the set of beliefs are restricted to the small group of Jawoyn who are entrusted with sacred knowledge.[1] According to Jawoyn tradition, people are bodily and morally identified with their country and with the ancestral being Bula. In the Creation era, Bula was associated with a more powerful female sea entity called Yingarna. The myths trace the journey of Bula from the sea to the Gimbat region, which includes Guratba. Bula was accompanied by his wives and by two men, Brown Goshawk and Plains Kangaroo. They fashioned the landscape, creating the country, raising the rocky hills and laying down the rivers. Bula also met and sat with the Rainbow Serpent. Bula went first to Nilaynjurrung (Big Sunday) and then to other sites before entering the earth to remain peacefully unless disturbed. Bula is now said to live at various interconnected sites in the area.

The country of the Jawoyn is imbued with the bodily 'essence' of Bula, a concept that has both a physical aspect and 'an inner property which is outwardly manifested, such as the glow of a diffused light'.[2] The term used by the Jawoyn for Bula's bodily essence, *ngan-mol*, is also used to refer to the minerals that white people mine. The gold in Coronation Hill is seen as the blood of Bula, so that to mine the ore is to disturb Bula himself.

It is said that Jawoyn men sing songs near the Bula sites in order to ward off danger. Ceremonies to renew the land were once performed. Older men recall avoidance and behavioural rules for people in the vicinity of the sites. Women, children and young men are excluded from the focal area of each Bula site. The Jawoyn believe that people are directly and morally connected to Bula through their own bodies and that if disturbed Bula has the power to inflict great harm on people. Bula can destroy the whole country through floods and fires and earthquakes.

The Bula myth has always been the focus of morality and connectedness in Jawoyn society. In former times and still today, older people told stories that were ethical tales inspired by the need to teach correct ways to live; the Bula tradition was 'a sustaining image of power and authority beyond human control'.[3]

THE DISPUTE AT CORONATION HILL

In the political domain, opposition to mining at Coronation Hill was originally motivated by concerns about the impact of mining on the natural environment of the area. Since Coronation Hill lies on the headwaters of the South Alligator River, environmentalists were concerned that the river system which supports the whole of the Kakadu region could be damaged by leaching from waste rock dumps or by spillages of cyanide or petroleum into the river. In addition, there would be unavoidable damage to the area around the hill both from the mining operation and from the greatly increased human presence including new roads and camps for mine workers.

The area surrounding Coronation Hill has been degraded by the introduction of domesticated hoofed animals (Australia has no native hoofed animals) and this led to the area being described by the much-quoted, but profoundly misleading, epithet 'clapped-out buffalo country'. However, the area has resumed much of its original character with the eradication of buffalo and its management as a conservation reserve. The headwaters of the South Alligator River provide the habitat for a rich variety of wildlife. Some of these creatures—such as the Kakadu dunnart, the pig-nosed turtle and the red goshawk— are rare or endangered.

Coronation Hill was mined for uranium in the 1950s and a small pit remains high up on the side of the hill. Geologists have discovered commercial quantities of gold, platinum and palladium buried in Coronation Hill. Proven reserves, mostly of gold, are worth around $500 million. The proposed gold mine would have meant digging up and processing virtually the entire hill.

To the mining company and its supporters in the business community and the government, digging up Coronation Hill made very good economic sense, particularly as the Resource Assessment Commission concluded that the risk of a serious impact on the South Alligator ecosystem (other than the hill itself) would be very small. The international gold market was buoyant, profits would be good and Australia needed the export revenue. Although the Resource Assessment Commission showed that the net benefits to Australia from the mine—the value of the gold and other minerals less the costs involved in extracting them—amounted to only about $80 million, why would anyone want to stop a mining development that would provide a badly needed stimulus to the national and local economies, including employment for otherwise unemployed Jawoyn, tax revenue for the government and profits for the shareholders?

To most of the Jawoyn, the issues were very different. Guratba, Coronation Hill, is a sacred place, repository of the bodily essence of the creator being Bula. While in Jawoyn cosmology Guratba is not the most sacred place in the region, a status reserved for Nilaynjurrung (Big Sunday) and Ngartluk (Sleisbeck), it is nevertheless dangerous and has to be treated with respect. The attitude of the Jawoyn to mining at Guratba can only be appreciated by understanding and accepting the personal significance of the Bula legend to the Jawoyn and their society.

TWO WORLDVIEWS

Clearly, there were fundamental differences between the mining company's perception of the situation and that of the Jawoyn Aborigines. The confrontation over mining at Coronation Hill expressed the most profound difference in perceptions of what we are as humans and our relationship to the world. At their core, the arguments of those in favour of mining reflect the radical division in Western thinking between the individual and the external world, between the observer and the observed, the actor and the acted upon. That distinction is the starting point of Western scientific rational thinking and requires some explanation.

In the Western mode of self-perception, which is expressed in its starkest form in modern economics, we are defined by our individuality. We think of ourselves as being independent components of the world in which we live. We are the active subjects and the world is the object of our actions. This perception was firmly planted in the Western mind during the European Enlightenment and represented a wholly new way of perceiving ourselves. It found its most clear expression in nineteenth-century Newtonian science and the philosophy of René Descartes. This worldview has been adopted uncritically by modern economics. The sharp distinction between the observer and the observed is expressed in economics by the archetypal situation in which the economic agent, known as *homo economicus*, confronts the material environment. *Homo economicus* acts on the physical world, which now consists of 'resources', in order to satisfy human desires. In no sense does *homo economicus* participate in the world. Unlike in other modes of self-awareness, the world is essentially dead. In other societies, historically and in places still today, the world is a pulsating organism fraught with meaning and intentions.

Today, then, we approach the world with a consciousness of non-participation (to use Morris Berman's phrase). This has enormous implications for the way we see the world and act on it. It determines our attitudes to the natural world. Because we view ourselves as radically separate from it, the natural environment takes on value only to the extent that it satisfies human needs and desires. This is the explicit assumption of economics in which 'goods' have value only to the extent that people are willing to trade them in the marketplace. The natural environment becomes a collection of more or less tradable resources.

The separation of our selves as beings from the natural world has meant that our attitudes to the environment are wholly different to those of peoples whose cultures and modes of awareness grew out of the land. Since the Industrial Revolution in Europe, European attitudes have been built on a one-way relationship of exploitation in which we have unilaterally assumed a moral right to take from the land without a reciprocal obligation to nurture it. This is worlds away from the attitude of indigenous cultures in which it is felt that the support that the natural world provides to their survival must be balanced by nurturing and recreating the land each day. In this way there is a mutually sustaining cycle between humans and their natural world just as there is for each creature that plays its own unique role in the reproduction of the cosmic cycle.

Joseph Campbell recounts a powerful myth of the Blackfoot, a Native American tribe, that illustrates the relationship of mutual support very forcefully.[4] Survival for the Blackfoot tribe depended on the winter supply of meat from buffaloes which they killed by driving them over a cliff. The story is told of how, during a time of hunger for the tribe, a young Blackfoot woman offered herself in marriage to the great bull of the buffalo herd if some of the buffaloes would sacrifice themselves to feed the tribe. Some of the buffaloes complied by throwing themselves over the cliff and the bull took the now-reluctant young woman away. When the young woman's father came to rescue her from the buffalo camp he was caught and trampled to pieces. Through her cries of grief the woman heard the great bull say "Now you know what we feel when your tribe kills our fathers and sisters and children". But he took pity on her and promised that if she could bring her father back to life, they could both return to their tribe. From a remaining piece of her father the young woman sang a song that brought him back to life. The great bull was amazed at her powers. But before they were allowed to leave the great bull taught father and daughter the sacred song and dance of the buffalo. Thereafter, the Blackfoot always performed the buffalo ritual after a kill in order to bring the buffalo back to life.

Through this ritual the Blackfoot psychologically recreated the natural world to keep it, and thus themselves, from permanent damage. They did not selfishly snatch their food from an unresponsive and inert natural world, a world in which survival occurs at the expense of the sources of life. The buffaloes they killed sacrificed themselves to the Blackfoot so that the latter could survive and in return the Blackfoot honoured their benefactors and took care not to take more than they needed. The people and their natural world formed an organic unity based on mutual respect, a relationship that created an ecological harmony.

The wholesale slaughter of the buffalo by white hunters in the 1870s and 1880s meant to the North American plains tribes far more than the loss of their principal source of food. The myths that established the relationship between the tribes and their animal sources of survival were the religious symbols that sustained their societies and their psychological selves.

> Hence, with the buffalo gone, the binding symbol was gone. Within the span of a decade the religion had become archaic; and it was then that the peyote cult, the mescal cult, came pouring up from Mexico . . . .[5]

By taking the peyote buttons the plains tribes hoped to find 'within themselves what had been lost from their society, namely an imagery of holiness, giving depth, psychological security, and apparent meaning to their lives'.

Similarly, the separation of Australian Aborigines from their country was far more than a change in their means of livelihood. The relationship to the land was one that sustained them not only physically but psychologically and spiritually. The opposition by the Jawoyn to mining at Coronation Hill thus expressed a wholly different perception of the world, a world in which humans and their environment form a unity. The Bula legend both expresses and reaffirms that unity, dissolving the distinction between self and other, creating the bond between the Jawoyn and their country.

The Jawoyn and other indigenous people retain a cosmology; the purpose of a cosmology is to provide an understanding of the nature of existence and to express the relationship felt by people towards their origins and their natural environment. For the Jawoyn, their cosmology, in which Bula is the central figure, is inseparable from the notion of 'country'. According to Stanner,

Our word 'home', warm and suggestive though it be, does not match the Aboriginal word that may mean 'camp', 'hearth', 'country', 'everlasting home', 'totem place', 'life source', 'spirit centre' and much else all in one. Our word 'land' is too spare and meagre. We can now scarcely use it except with economic overtones unless we happen to be poets . . . . A different tradition leaves us tongueless and earless towards this other world of meaning and significance. When we took what we call 'land' we took what to them meant hearth, home, the source and locus of life, and everlastingness of spirit.[6]

The Bula tradition is not so much a means of making a link between subject and object, for there is no separation; it is an expression of their unity. Jawoyn cosmology, like that of mystics the world over (including Europe), simply expresses the primordial unity of human and universal consciousness, the absence of boundaries.

The imagery is uncommonly explicit in the Bula tradition. People are actually connected to Bula through their bodily essences. Through this connection 'Bula' can know the actions and thoughts of the people and punish those who transgress. The sickness and injuries that befall the transgressor are explained in the Western tradition as random accidents, the result of meeting a germ or just being careless. For the Jawoyn, people are directly and 'morally' connected with Bula through their own bodies. The sacred sites where Bula or his essence lie are believed to be linked to each Jawoyn by means of 'wires' or 'strings' in such a way that Bula can keep track of them and monitor their activities[7]. Clearly, these 'strings' are metaphorical but the relationship is no less real for that. The Jawoyn connection with Bula is an unusually literal rendering of a primordial form of consciousness that has characterised societies and individuals in all ages in all parts of the world.

A NEW AUSTRALIAN DREAMING

The contrast between the Jawoyn view of Coronation Hill and the mining company's perception could not be more stark. White Australia's attitude to the land was formed in the early years of settlement. The settlers were confronted with an alien and hostile land. Convicts and soldiers were drawn from the urban underclasses of Britain, people who had already lost their links with the soil. For survival, the earth had to be tamed. The spiritual alienation wrought by the European Enlightenment and the Scientific Revolution found its most fertile ground in communities that had been formed in isolation from their spiritual roots.

What we see today in place of the human spirit united with the natural world is an economist, an economist within each of us. This 'rational economic man' is often presented, to others and to ourselves, as no more than someone who wants to get ahead or to have a bit of security. Sometimes this acquisitive character may be concealed by layer upon layer of traits that are precisely the opposite. The selfish calculator is the 'economic agent' of the economic rationalists who is believed to capture our real motivations. In recent years more and more government policy has been based explicitly on the economists' view of what drives us as humans. But while *homo economicus* lurks within all of us it is not our true self and only takes us away from real contentment. Deep down we all know this.

In the face of the profound clash of world views, the Hawke Government's decision in 1991 to prevent mining at Coronation Hill was one of enormous symbolic significance. It was met with deep incomprehension and unrelenting rage on the part of the mining industry and its supporters, for it seemed to challenge the most fundamental principles on which the industry, and indeed the whole economy and society, were built. But the decision to prevent mining penetrated even deeper into the Australian psyche. White Australia was a society formed by tearing Europeans from their roots. On the journey to Australia, the European dreaming was left behind. The dreaming is the stuff of Carl Jung's 'collective unconscious', the repository of myths, legends and archetypes that order our lives and provide a focus and a meaning for existence. They may take centuries to form and crystalize. For white Australia the psychological tumult of leaving Europe meant that the tradition was not passed on—there was, as it were, a break in the song line. In recent years there have been signs in Australia, as elsewhere in the West, of a recognition that we as a people are missing the things that matter most. The environment movement is an expression of this, a groping for some means, some way of life, some dream that will allow us to reestablish that sense of unity with the whole that Bula still seems to provide for the Jawoyn.

Though white Australia tore Aborigines from their land—their country, their hearth, their very source of life—and threw their societies into appalling decline, Aboriginal communities like the Jawoyn clung to their dreaming in an attempt to avoid the spiritual emptiness that ravaged white society. The decision to prevent mining at Coronation Hill was a victory for the remnant strength of the Aboriginal dreaming over the need of white society to satisfy, by material acquisition, its ravening spiritual hunger. But it was also a victory for the embryonic resurgence of a new dreaming in white Australia and can only signify the beginning of a return to psychological health.

1 The principal source for the background to and significance of the Bula tradition is the report by Ian Keen and Francesca Merlan, 'The Significance of the Conservation Zone to Aboriginal People', Resource Assessment Commission Consultancy Series (AGPS, Canberra, December 1990). I am indebted to Barbara Lepani for stimulating many of the ideas in this essay.

2 Keen and Merlan, *ibid.*, p. 44

3 See Keen and Merlan, *ibid.*, pp. 25-26

4 Joseph Campbell, *Myths to Live By* (Bantam Books, New York 1973) pp. 37-40

5 Campbell, *ibid.*, p. 89

6 W. Stanner, *White Man Got No Dreaming* (ANU Press, Canberra 1979)

7 See Keen and Merlan, *op. cit.*, p. 47

5 MONEY AND WORK: SACRED OR SECULAR?

EMPTINESS AND MONEY

Depression is a common experience for people in Western societies. It is often associated with a feeling of meaninglessness in our lives, a sense of 'what's the point' and an awareness rarely understood or acknowledged that we have no proper home on the Earth. These feelings are something we often find embarrassing to admit in a social milieu where life is supposed to be an endless round of good times. Although it is very hard to put a finger on it, many now question the authenticity of their lives—of their work, their personal relationships, their relationships to themselves. Many people report experiencing a feeling of a great void or emptiness within, as if they are only a physical shell going through daily life according to habit. Many of us have experienced times in our lives when we have felt abandoned in the world, isolated in a hostile place, even though we are in our home town and may have a secure family to return to. Some people walk the Earth with the fear that if they look too closely at themselves, at their origins and their futures, they will find that there is nothing there, that they do not exist.

In an attempt to recapture the meaning that is missing in an alienated life many people respond by going shopping. Shopping, especially for items other than our daily needs, is an activity that has a range of powerful associations that have seeped into our consciousnesses. We are schooled in a thousand subtle ways to feel that to possess is to capture power; indeed, that possessions are the essential source of power in our society. There is a subconscious association which tells us that if we have power over goods we will have power over life, at least over our own lives. This expresses our need to overcome our essential powerlessness in mass societies which rob us of the sense of true community and the opportunity to express ourselves as we truly are rather than as mere personas in search of social acceptance.

If shopping has become the activity by which we try to give meaning to our lives, then the shopping malls which now embellish every city are the shrines we build to this power. On the face of it, shopping malls are no more than a convenient way to have access to a variety of services. But there is a powerful psychology to the shopping mall. Unlike the traditional market, the bazaar or even the suburban high street, shopping malls are devoted exclusively to consumer activity, to spending money. The shopping mall feels quite different from the world outside. We enter a trance-like state when we enter a shopping mall, a sort of meditation in which the mantra that focuses our concentration is the promise of consumption. Our minds hum to the tune 'I can buy and possess'. The mall provides insulation against a hostile world. In a perverse way shopping malls are liberating; we feel that all of those goods, all of that power, are potentially there for us. But the freedom they appear to offer is a false freedom manufactured by the marketing society, one that we have absorbed from earliest childhood and one that ultimately yields no real satisfaction.

Shopping malls are deliberately uniform in character. This is very apparent when one walks off the streets of Bangkok or Mexico City into a shopping mall, streets which to a foreigner are filled with a sense of uniqueness and excitement. The malls feel so much like those in the West because they are designed to express one supreme activity, consumer spending.[1] Developing countries continue to absorb the definition of self of the West, a self in which shopping serves the dual purpose of allowing us to buy what we desire and of holding out the possibility of filling our empty lives with the hope of significance, a power that we attach to the spirit of the material goods that money can buy.

One powerful confirmation of this psychological function of the act of purchasing is the attitude we adopt to goods that we have acquired free of charge. Somehow we have less regard for freely-given goods than for goods we have acquired through spending our own money. When we spend our own money we feel that we are investing part of ourselves in the goods we buy, so that we can spread the power of our egos beyond the confines of our bodies. The devaluation of free goods is often overridden by other cultural norms or feelings, such as the satisfaction derived from eating something grown by oneself. But in children it is quite apparent. Modern children have a craving for things that have been bought in a shop. Meals cooked at home, clothes sewn at home and toys made at home lack the magic of consumption. Children learn that a thing they have saved their own money to buy or a thing for which their parents have 'sacrificed' their money has enormous value; it gives them a taste of the personal power conferred by purchasing power.

The traditional high street or bazaar served more purposes than simply providing a place to shop. It was a meeting place; it had the feel of neighbourliness; it expressed a sense of community as well as a sense of commerce. Even today these feelings can be recaptured in 'alternative markets'; we go there as citizens as well as consumers. They acknowledge the social being, even the spiritual being, as well as the economic being. The shopping mall has none of this; its sole function is to sell and in so doing it strives to give meaning to our lives. I am because I consume. Contradictory as it may seem, shopping is an attempt to recapture a sense of community. Fox and Lears trace the changes in the social functions of consumption:

> Life for most middle-class and many working-class Americans in the twentieth century has been a ceaseless pursuit of the "good life" and a constant reminder of their powerlessness. . . . Although the dominant institutions of our culture have purported to be offering the consumer a fulfilling participation in the life of the community, they have to a large extent presented the empty prospect of taking part in the marketplace of personal exchange.[2]

People naturally pursue a sense of community, of belonging to a group, as well as a sense of belonging to the world. With the breakdown of old communities and the emergence of the economic individual under industrial capitalism, the new sense of society embraced whole countries rather than local communities. People began to perceive that the path to acceptability in the new society was to adopt, as always, the socially appropriate forms of behaviour. These new forms of behaviour stressed the importance of material acquisition and material comforts. Since everyone seemed to want this above all, acquisitiveness became the means of finding a sense of community. But what a lonely sense of community it turned out to be; it was to be had not by interacting with other people but by purchasing disembodied, impersonal products in the marketplace, as if by purchasing socially sanctioned goods we could buy a sense of belonging. Ignoring those around us, we came to look for a sense of community on the shelves of the supermarkets.

The urge to shop is an attempt at self-definition in an age of anonymity that seems to deprive us of a place in the world, a sense of self that the close-knit communities of old could provide. In the vast urban dormitories of today there is a desperate need to define oneself by commodity display; the house and the car become essential to one's presentation to the world, and are the signals to which the world responds.[3] The communities of old could be savage in their stratification, sanctioning all manner of exploitation. The consumer identity of modern market capitalism with its promise of universal material well-being seemed to augur the end of social inequality. But the commodity self has failed, not only because exploitation persists but because the commodity self is not real. The outside world of the consuming self became divorced from the inner feeling self so that we now suffer from terminal anomie.

The apparent ability of money to give meaning to our lives is exploited ruthlessly by those who sell consumer credit. Advertisements for consumer credit make the clear statement that we, the consumer, can have the life that we want by spending money on consumer goods—cars, boats, caravans, appliances—and they, the credit-givers, can give us access to those goods. We now have a proliferation of social welfare agencies and programmes designed to deal with the social and family problems that consumer debt generates. In an era in the West of ever-greater material wealth and of ever-greater spiritual impoverishment and meaninglessness, it is little wonder that consumer debt has grown at explosive rates. In an attempt to give meaning to our increasingly meaningless lives we have accumulated more and more debt.

Shopping is a response to our existential depression, when the world seems to overwhelm us, when we feel we have been put on the earth only to drag ourselves through a life of drudgery. Fleetingly, we can break out and revolt by going shopping. Shopping is even tinged by a sense of challenge to the world, to the lives we are stuck in; it is a rebuke to the system that tries to engulf us. 'I can't afford it but, damn it, I'll buy it anyway.' Ultimately, though, shopping can be no release; it can only enmesh us further. The fleeting sense of power that comes with a purchase only leaves a greater void to be filled. It is like struggling to get out of quick sand—struggling like this we only sink deeper into the mire. In the last instance, to consume is to concede defeat; to consume like this is slowly to die.

The cry for riches to fill the existential void is not of course a wholly modern phenomenon. For centuries it has been understood that the hope invested in material wealth can only turn into greater hope, leaving happiness a dream. Goethe knew:

> Blundering with desire towards fruition,
>
> And in fruition pining for desire.[4]

But whereas this form of futile activity was reserved for the few in previous ages, today it is the fate of the mass of ordinary people.

While the personal evidence of the futility of material acquisitiveness mounts we continue to be assailed at every point in every day of our lives by messages that affirm the power of money. The power of money is true enough; those with money are powerful in Western society. But they are powerful in the particular sense of having control over material resources, and over other people. Those who are driven to ever greater accumulation of things are driven by inner urges and unmet needs which they neither control nor understand.

GOLD AND IMMORTALITY

There is no denying that money gives us power over things and other people. But the satisfaction from that power is only fleeting; and we know underneath that it is a false power, one that cannot give us what we truly want. I will argue that what we truly want is to transcend the division between ourselves and the universe, to attain the godhead and achieve immortality, but that we attempt to attain it by false means, by money. It is impossible to buy transcendence, but the attempt to make money the link between ourselves and the divine gives it enormous symbolic power.

The essence of money lies not in its function as a means of exchange but in its function as a store of value, congealed power. As Norman Brown tells us: 'The ultimate category of economics is power; but power is not an economic category. . . . all power is essentially sacred power'.[5] We pursue transcendence, and we are led by our egos to believe that the road to it lies in the world of economics, the metamorphosis of the sacred.

The exchange function of money that distinguishes the official economic treatment of it is a pallid explanation indeed. An understanding of its real magical function lurks in all of us, and sometimes it is found particularly in the understanding of the poor who do not need to overlay their understanding with rationalisations that justify possession of large quantities of it. Ernest Becker quotes the formulation of Geza Roheim: 'originally people do not desire money because you can buy things for it, but you can buy things for money because people desire it'.[6] Of course, economics maintains precisely the opposite; money is no more than a means of exchange; economies are essentially big barter systems made more convenient by the mediatory function of money. Money simply oils the wheels of commerce. The great French economist Leon Walras, one of the founders of modern neoclassical economics and remembered for his remarkable system of general economic equilibrium, invented the device of the grand auctioneer who stands in the middle of a marketplace teeming with agents who are each simultaneously buyers and sellers. The auctioneer clears the market by taking bids from buyers up to the point where sellers agree to sell, a process known as *tatonnement*. Money is no more than a convenient device to achieve this.

While most ordinary people believe that economics is about money, the economy of the economists is essentially moneyless; the principles of the microeconomics textbooks can be fully elaborated without the intervention of money. The use of money in actual economies is portrayed as little more than a practical device for efficiently effecting exchanges. To be sure, money is typically attributed the additional function of acting as a store of value, as well as being a medium of exchange; but a store of value is here only an exchange delayed. Thus throughout the history of neoclassical economics, money is barely mentioned. In neoclassical theory, money becomes a significant economic influence only when governments fail to understand that money is no more than a device to facilitate exchange and as a result print too much of it. Then money becomes a means of redistributing wealth and a source of economic instability. Now a theory of money and of macroeconomics becomes necessary, especially when combined with private money-producing institutions such as banks which can create credit beyond the demands of the system of exchange of goods.

The greatness of J. M. Keynes, now somewhat faded after some two decades of sustained attack from the free market purists, lay in his early intuition that money was a force of its own. His *magnum opus* was called *The General Theory of Employment, Interest and Money*. The earlier work that provided all of the foundations for it was entitled simply *A Treatise on Money*. In the 1970s, the most influential response to Keynes took the form of 'monetarism', associated most strongly with the name of Milton Freidman, the burden of which was to reassert the powerless of money in a properly regulated economy. If the government understood the proper function of money, it was argued, and only created as much as the economy demanded, money would revert to its natural wheel-oiling function. Monetarism in the 1970s and early 1980s became the focus of a broad reassertion of the power of the free market, and was closely aligned with a new brand of right-wing economic liberalism. Freidman was rewarded with a Nobel Prize for his monetarist work.

Economists have assumed that the 'economic' activities of traditional societies can be separated out as islands of self-interested rationality in a sea of superstition. Modern economies then can be seen as a simple expansion of the island of rationality to displace the sea. Anthropologists, however, agree that economic activity in traditional societies was 'submerged in "non-economic" relations; and they emphasize the ceremonial (ritual) character of these non-economic relations'.[7] We can agree with Brown when he argues that we have not witnessed the 'secularisation' of our social worlds, including the economy, but merely the 'metamorphosis of the sacred'.[8] We are still driven by the same basic motive—to deny death, to overcome the terror that our inescapable mortality imposes on us. As Ernest Becker tells us, money

> is still sacred, still a magical object on which we rely for our entrance into immortality. . . . Gold became the new immortality symbol. . . . the cosmic powers could be the property of everyman . . . you could now traffic for immortality in the marketplace.[9]

The difference in the new world was that substitution of money-power for the fruits of ritual carried with it the privatisation of access to the sacred.

What is it then that at the deepest level still motivates us today endlessly to pursue more? Ernest Becker provides us with an answer and, if we accept that what humans really want is transcendence, it should not surprise us to learn that the motivation was, and remains, essentially religious.

> . . . primitive man created an economic surplus so that he would have something to give to the gods; . . . to keep the cycle of power moving from the invisible to the visible world.[10]

Consciousness is humankind's great opportunity as well as its burden. We are condemned to contemplate our mortality yet we are granted the possibility of transcending the mundane world. Surplus, expansion, growth and their essential material form, money, are our characteristic means to bridge 'the aching gap between what I know and what I am'.[11] Becker is well worth quoting again:

> Man, the animal who knows he is not safe here, who needs continued affirmation of his powers, is the one animal who is implacably driven to work beyond animal needs precisely because he is not a secure animal. The origin of human drivenness is religious because man experiences creatureliness; the amassing of a surplus, then, goes to the very heart of human motivation, the urge to stand out as a hero, to transcend the limitations of the human condition and achieve victory over impotence and finitude.[12]

As the agricultural surpluses were produced each year and began to circulate, money came to embody the power of the surpluses. Money could be transformed into surplus, surplus into money, so that money itself came to represent the power of immortality attained by appeasing the gods. Whereas in older cultures transactions with the gods were conducted by way of ritual, and all of life's activities were liturgical, money 'filled the vacuum left by ritual and itself became the new ritual focus'.[13] And although we imagine ourselves to have lifted our minds above the level of superstitious ritual as a means of remaining in touch with the other world, we have not changed at our deepest levels.

This is why money is so powerful in our society. Its symbolic power is immense. Money can have such power only because it holds out the promise of immortality, the ability to transcend insignificance and powerlessness. We no longer offer up the surplus to the gods; the accumulation of money itself is our god.

If gold replaced ritual as the currency of transcendence, we can understand the historical fact that the first banks were temples and the first issuers of money were priests.

> The first mints were set up in the temples of the gods, whence our word "money"—from the mint in the temple of Juno Moneta, Juno the Admonisher, on the Capitoline Hill in Rome. Forgery was sacrilege because the coins embodied the powers of the gods and only the priests could handle such powers . . . .[14]

Just as those who controlled ritual in older societies could wield great power over others, now those who hold the keys to the bank vaults hold control over the essence of every citizen's desires, and thus of Western civilization.

It took many centuries for the sacredness of money to replace other forms of religious striving. It reached its zenith with the rise and dominance of industrial capitalism in Western Europe. In this sense then, the power of money is a very modern phenomenon. In pre-capitalist Europe, political power attached to birth rather than wealth, although it was part of the process to use one's power of birth to amass a fortune. The rich merchants had far less power than their money would confer on them today. We have become so accustomed to the social power of money that we believe that it is the natural state of the world. But the cultural specificity of money's power can still be observed. The close Western association between wealth and power is contradicted in some Third World cultures, especially those which have a strong caste system. For a Western observer walking a Himalayan track, it is immensely puzzling to see a wealthy but lower-caste man humble himself in the presence of ragged and destitute but high-caste Brahmin. We are so accustomed to associating wealth with prestige and standing, and so committed to our personal 'dignity', that a social system such as that of Nepal is beyond our comprehension.

The social function of the power of money was particularly apparent to observers of society in the period of transition from feudalism to capitalism. Karl Marx was one of the most acute observers of the change, even though capitalism was fully dominant, in Britain at least, at the time of his writing. In the *Economic and Philosophic Manuscripts of 1844*, Marx wrote of the power of money in the new society in the following terms:

> The extent of the power of money is my power. Money's properties are my properties and essential powers—the properties and powers of its possessor. . . . I am ugly, but I can buy for myself the most beautiful of women. Therefore I am not ugly, for the effect of ugliness—its deterrent power—is nullified by money. I, in my character as an individual, am lame, but money furnishes me with twenty-four feet. Therefore I am not lame. I am bad, dishonest, unscrupulous, stupid; but money is honoured, and therefore so is its possessor. Money is the supreme good, therefore its possessor is good. Money, besides, saves me the trouble of being dishonest: I am therefore presumed honest. I am stupid, but money is the real mind of all things and how then should its possessor be stupid? Besides, he can buy talented people for himself, and is he who has power over the talented not more talented than the talented? Do not I, who thanks to money am capable of all that the human heart longs for, possess all human capacities? Does not my money therefore transform all my incapacities into their contrary?[15]

But even before the emergence of industrial society the corrupting power of money was a common theme. In *Timon of Athens*, Shakespeare wrote this of money:

> Gold? Yellow, glittering, precious gold? No, Gods, I am no idle votarist! . . . Thus much of this will make black white, foul fair,
> Wrong right, base noble, old young, coward valiant.
> . . . Why, this

Will lug your priests and servants from your sides,
Pluck stout men's pillows from below their heads:
This yellow slave
Will knit and break religions, bless th'accurst;
Make the hoar leprosy ador'd, place thieves
And give them title, knee and approbation
With senators on the bench: this is it
That makes the wappen'd widow wed again;
She, whom the spital-house and ulcerous sores
Would cast the gorge at, this embalms and spices
To th'April day again. Come, damned earth,
Thou common whore of mankind, that putt'st odds
Among the rout of nations.

(Act 4, Scene 3)

The power of money serves to convince us that it is not money that gives its possessor all of these human qualities of beauty, honour, talent and so on; the owner of money is beguiled into believing that the possession of these qualities empowers the possessor to acquire money. Sometimes recognition of this breaks through. For several decades in the early part of the twentieth century the idea of social equality became a powerful political force. It was motivated by residual ideas of *noblesse oblige* on the part of the wealthy and Fabian morality on the part of the political representatives of the working class. More recently, Western society, spurred on by the cybernetic vision of economic rationalism, has been increasingly dominated by the view that those who are rich have earned their wealth by their special efforts or talents and that any attempt to redistribute some of their wealth to the poor is a denial of natural justice. Much is made of the 'self-made' entrepreneurs who have struggled their way up from penury. It is conveniently forgotten that the vast bulk of personal wealth is inherited.

THE WORTHLESSNESS OF MONEY

Researchers into folklore and psychology have observed that what is most worthless is often associated with what is most valuable. Nietzsche had the phrase: 'Out of the lowest the highest reaches its peak', which describes precisely the full circle of the alchemist's opus.[16] Many have been startled and puzzled by Christ's saying 'Look under a rock and you will find me there'. Brown suggests that money represents our animal natures, the mortal body. Money indeed is a means to immortality. If money is an attempt to rise above the body, it is premissed on the separation of mind and body and affirms the Enlightenment's neurotic vision, a mind 'freed' from the shackles of prosaic, mortal existence. The human mind can soar to higher things by separating itself from and denying its animal nature and especially its body.[17]

Whatever the psychological truth behind the mind-body split, it is clear that money is a great deal more than the neutral device perfectly suited to effect the circulation of goods that economics would have us believe. Popular culture and the poets have always known the essential worthlessness of money and, by extension, the futility of the acquisition of material goods. That would concur with our own deep recognition that money, other than providing for the basic necessities of life, does not bring happiness. Some philosophies acknowledge this fact explicitly. In the Zen Buddhist view, contentment comes from inner harmony and acceptance. Swami Muktananda, a master of Siddha yoga, expressed it this way:

> This is how a person lives. Lacking knowledge of the Truth, he chooses things according to his own interests without understanding whether they are good or bad for him. All his life his interests continually change according to his whims, which indicates that he never really finds what he wants.[18]

The ultimate impotence of money as a means of achieving contentment is a constant theme in classical and popular culture, from the Bible's 'For what shall it profit a man, if he shall gain the whole world, and lose his own soul?'[19] to Goethe's *Faust* to the Beatles' 'Money Can't Buy Me Love'. Dickens' *A Christmas Carol* is one of the most explicit and powerful statements of the theme. Scrooge, the quintessential miser, is dragged by the ghosts of Christmas (his unconscious needs that he has wholly repressed) through scenes which show happiness among material poverty (the London poor), happiness that springs from family closeness (the Cratchit family), happiness from gaiety, spontaneity and magic (his own childhood), happiness from shared experience and companionship (the Christmas streets) and happiness from the ability to feel compassion (for Tiny Tim). Scrooge is finally compelled to admit that his conscious obsession with money has repressed and imprisoned his essential human needs. The enduring popularity of the story confirms the fact that we recognise the conflict within Scrooge to be a conflict within each of us.

Despite the fact that we recognise the futility of material pursuits, our culture is built on the pursuit of happiness through material acquisition. The rich are revered yet also reviled. The popular press displays an untiring obsession with the affairs of the very rich, an obsession which reflects the fascination of the less well-endowed. Most of all we love to read about the tragedies of their personal lives as if constantly to reaffirm our understanding that wealth is not the path to personal contentment. We envy the rich for their wealth and admire their glamorous lifestyles, yet we know at a deeper level that, like Faust, they have sacrificed their souls in their pursuit of material things.

> In vain I gathered human treasure,
> And all that mortal spirit could digest:
> I come at last to recognize my measure,
> And know the sterile desert in my breast.[20]

The essential psychological conflict within modern Western society is the conflict between our unceasing, obsessive pursuit of material wealth and a deeper knowledge that this pursuit cannot bring us happiness, that (in Wilber's terminology) our 'Atman projects' cannot deliver us to 'Atman'. The conflict imposes a determining neurosis on society as a whole. The pursuit of material wealth is fundamentally an egotistical pursuit and is predicated on the emergence of individual thinking. It is as if having renounced our unity with the world we attempt to compensate by acquiring power over more and more of it. Acquisitiveness is individual; contentment grows from acceptance that we are important only through our participation in the whole. Economics, as always, looks only at the superficial appearances of things. Starting from the individual, the desire for material possessions becomes the central object of study of economics. We will see next that just as the consumption activity of humans takes on a distorted appearance in economics, so the productive activity, human labour, appears in economics, and in the world, in an alien form, reflecting no more than the surface appearances of actual individual behaviour.

The rationality of economics is intimately bound up with the rationality of money and the 'rationality' of money is only a metaphor of the sacred. In his examination of the psychology of modern society, Brown observes that

> money reflects and promotes a style of thinking which is abstract, impersonal, objective, and quantitative, that is to say, the style of thinking of modern science—and what could be more rational than that?[21]

While this style of thinking may sometimes be apparent in the world of business investment, banking and accounting, in the discipline of economics it has been elevated to imperial status. It is expressed in the concept of 'rigour', a complex of ideas associated with rationality, abstraction, exclusion of emotion and, usually, mathematical sophistication. The highest praise that can be given to an economist's work is to describe it as rigorous.

While the money economy has been with us for many centuries, the complete domination of economic activity by monetary transactions was a product of the Industrial Revolution and the associated division of labour. It was only with the enormous advances in productive potentialities ushered in by the Industrial Revolution that it became possible for entire populations to risk abandoning subsistence farming and to trust their fate to the vagaries of highly specialised wage labour. The development of factory labour and urbanisation opened up the possibility—realised in the West in the decades since the Second World War—of whole societies devoting themselves to consumption as an end in itself, as a means of affirming the worth of individuals. The dominance of analytical rationality has been one of the central psychological correlates of these changes.

Economics has not constructed the notion of rational economic man from nothing, but has built its economic agent from observation of the way we appear to behave. We all carry *homo economicus* around with us in our heads. Our social conditioning provides us with this idea as a guide to the way we think about ourselves and the world around us. Although we are cast in chains by a social system and our egos, we fall in love with our chains. But *homo economicus* is a distorted view of ourselves; our abstract, impersonal, objective, and quantitative style of thinking grows out of the confrontation between our true human natures and the social forces to which we must adapt as we mature. Even money itself is not the secular, rational, wholly external object that it appears to be. The anthropological roots of money reveal its continuing magical or sacred character.[22] As a final illustration, Keynes, among others, noted that the attraction of gold and silver lay in their symbolic identification with the Sun and the Moon. In Latin America gold and silver appear in folklore as the sweat of the sun and the tears of the moon. Moreover, in Europe from ancient times to around 1880, the ratio of the value of gold to that of silver was purposefully set at 1:13.5, a ratio which bore no relation to the relative quantities of gold and silver supplied and demanded but which was set by the astrological ratio of the annual cycles of their divine counterparts, the Sun and the Moon. That is, there were 13.5 parts of silver to one part of gold because there are 13.5 lunar cycles for each annual solar cycle.

WORK, TIME AND ALIENATION

What is the distinction between life and work? Why does the economic analysis of household behaviour begin from the 'disutility', that is, the unpleasantness, of work? Is there something intrinsic to work that makes it unpleasant? These are questions of acute importance not only for our society but for each of us individually.

The transformation of work in industrial societies has been intimately related to the transformation of our perceptions of time. In traditional societies mythic time was cyclical, periodic, ahistorical; time revolved and returned, reflecting the rhythms of life-activity and the sacred cosmology that gave the mythic mind its gods and archetypes. Modern time is linear, continuous and irreversible, the substance from which we construct the idea of history and with which we extrapolate into the future. In traditional societies time did not stand apart from humankind, promising the inevitability of death, but was interwoven with the cycle of life. The alchemists stood halfway between the archaic and the modern. Their opus was to change Nature by producing gold from base metals and in this they were aware that they entered into the domain of time.

> [I]n taking upon himself the responsibility of changing Nature, man put himself in the place of Time; that which would have required millennia or aeons to 'ripen' in the depths of the earth, the metallurgist and alchemist claim to be able to achieve in a few weeks. The furnace supersedes the telluric matrix; it is there that the embryo-ores complete their growth.[23]

Traditionally, everything in the world was believed to evolve, even metals under the earth. But this idea of evolution meant something quite different to the modern idea of 'progress'. Progress, an idea which has powerful emotional content and which invades our every thought, is a product of human intervention. In a compelling argument, Eliade maintains that it is in the Industrial Revolution, with its compulsion to dominate and transform Nature, that we find 'the authentic continuation of the alchemist's dream'.

> The visionary's myth of the perfection, or more accurately, of the redemption of Nature, survives, in camouflaged form, in the pathetic programme of the industrial societies whose aim is the total transmutation of Nature, its transformation into 'energy'.[24]

In this programme, 'rational economic man' finally succeeds in supplanting time. After millennia of stasis, humanity has in a few decades transformed the substances of the Earth so as to multiply its products thousands of times over. Indeed, and more importantly, the parallel psychological shift saw humankind absorbed by the belief that the productivity of the Earth is limitless when combined with the technological products of the human mind. Such is progress, whose determining feature is the defeat of time. Technology and human labour substitute for time. In recent years, environmental catastrophes unfolding on the globe have forced more and more people to recognise the limits to the Earth's productive capacity. Consequently, we are beginning to rethink notions of progress, and perhaps of time.

In industrial society, work took on the role of time, but to do so work had to be transformed, a price had to be paid. 'To supply the necessary energy to the dreams and ambitions of the nineteenth century, work had to be secularized'.[25] The secularisation of work was imposed on working people by the early factory system. The dream of Infinite Progress, the mission of industrial society, was the dream of the new middle classes. The birth of the proletariat, who would carry through this dream, often had to be induced by legislated devices such as the enclosure laws which forced peasants from their land. The industrial working class was dragged from the already uncomfortable feudal womb by forceps of steel. Here more than ever work took on the character of disutility which pulls life down:

> it is in work finally secularized, in work in its pure state, numbered in hours and units of energy consumed, that man feels the implacable nature of temporal duration, its full weight and slowness.[26]

This is a grim historical truth that economists have canonised in eternal law. The dream of a machine-universe took concrete form in the early factories, where humans were not only thought of as cogs in a machine but were generally treated that way. The Taylorisation of work in the 1920s was an explicit attempt to dehumanise workers so that they functioned in the same way as the unerring machinery that regulated their labour. Taylorisation was the apotheosis of capitalist management practice. While the Taylorisation of work flourished in the 1920s, the essential principles remain embedded in the institutions of work today despite some recent trends towards humanising work.

The essential principles of Frederick Taylor's system of 'scientific management' have not been better stated than by Taylor himself.[27]

> First principle: 'The managers assume . . . the burden of gathering together all of the traditional knowledge which in the past has been possessed by the workmen . . . '
>
> Second principle: 'All possible brain work should be removed from the shop and centered in the planning or laying-out department . . . '
>
> Third principle: 'The work of every workman is fully planned out by the management . . . [and] specifies not only what is to be done, but how it is to be done and the exact time allowed for doing it . . . '

Taylorisation signalled not merely the end of participating consciousness at work, but, for the mass of factory workers, the end of deliberative thought as well.

The secularisation of work, of which Taylorisation was the finest hour, was the secularisation of life; it meant that we could no longer be redeemed by work. Labour was no longer liturgy and the creation of a surplus was no longer an offering to the gods. Work that was previously devotional became the means to the modern substitute for god, consumption. The purpose of work lay no longer in the activity itself but in the end product; the sacred function of work itself is transformed into its profane product.

It is in consumer products that we vainly invest our hope for immortality. While rational economic man, by assuming the role of time, took on the mantle of the alchemist, he simultaneously sloughed the sacred character of the alchemist's task. The alchemist's work, like that of the hunter and the farmer, remained the work of ritual; its purpose was in the practice rather than the product. To those who have managed some reintegration of the sacred into their lives, work still holds out the vestigial promise of fulfilment, of a celebration of Atman. But economics chooses again to hold up as the universal norm the alienated behaviour of a specific historical development. In the neoclassical theory of the 'labour market', work is a service provided by 'resource owners'. The work that we perform is analysed as a decision problem of choosing between two 'goods', the money income from labour and the 'psychic' income from leisure.

In Figure 3 our personal trade-offs between the income we would receive from working and the psychic income obtained from leisure are shown by the indifference curves I and I'. Each curve maps combinations of work and leisure between which we are indifferent. The 'budget line' B shows the hourly 'wage rate', which can be either the money income that can be had from each hour of labour or the psychic income to be had from each hour of leisure. The amount of labour a person 'supplies' (i.e. how much work they decide to do) depends on a comparison of the marginal utilities of leisure and income, and the wage rate.

Here is the economist's essential model of life. We can do no more than make a rational choice in which we weigh up the disutility of an extra hour of work against the utility to be had from spending, during our leisure time, the extra income earned in the previous hour. An equilibrium will emerge, a balance is struck, at which point we can be no happier. In this strange world, pleasure derives from the destruction of things (their

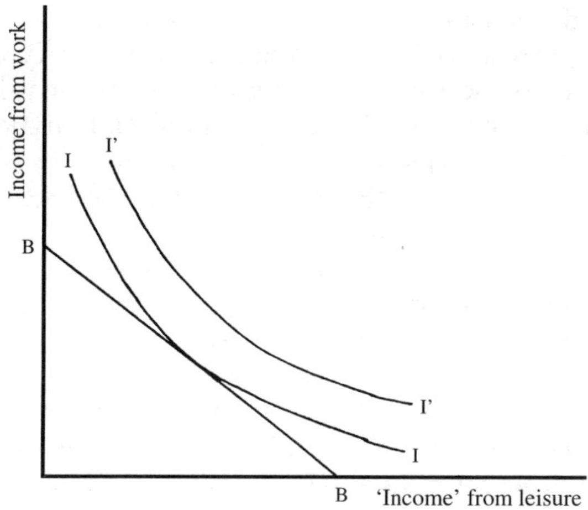

Figure 3 The trade-off between work and leisure

consumption) and displeasure from the creation of them (their production). To the modern economist there is no moral judgement in this; it is just how the world is. Yet every gardener knows that most of the pleasure is in the growing rather than the eating.

Although as a moral philosopher Adam Smith may have maintained that this is not how life is meant to be, it is perhaps in his famous example of the pin factory that the notion of the disutility of work originated. In Smith's pin factory each component of pin-making is classified, divided and allocated to a specialised worker. It was designed to illustrate the gains in productivity that specialisation and the division of labour could bring about. But it is rarely acknowledged by the economists that Smith himself recognised that specialisation through the division of labour not only has an enormous impact on the physical productivity of labour but also a debilitating psychological effect. A worker caught up in the detailed division of labour, observed Smith,

> becomes as stupid and ignorant as it is possible for a human creature to become . . . The torpor of his mind renders him, not only incapable of relishing or bearing a part in any rational conversation, but of conceiving any generous, noble, or tender sentiment, and consequently of forming any just judgment concerning many even of the

> ordinary duties of private life, . . . [or of the] great and extensive interests of his country. . . . His dexterity at his own particular trade seems, in this manner, to be acquired at the expense of his intellectual, social, and martial virtues.[28]

In pre-capitalist societies the idea of work as a means simply of earning income to buy the necessities of life was an alien one. Of course the compulsion to work to survive was overwhelming, especially in a feudal social structure where the penalties for failing to work were dire. But, except for those in relations of direct bondage, and even in the case of those, work was far more than a means to an end. Work was above all an expression of one's nature, the activity through which people entered into their environment and the cosmos. And since they experienced themselves as part of the world, work was the activity through which they regenerated themselves psychologically and spiritually.

The crippling of the intellect and the spirit was not only a result of the new factories; it was also a precondition for the survival and growth of the factory system. The traditional attitudes of the European peasantry and urban labouring classes were a definite constraint to the expansion of industrial enterprise. These attitudes, as Weber saw, were 'the greatest "inner obstacle" to the development of modern capitalism' and required a profound shift in the way people related to the means of material reproduction and, ultimately, in the definition of themselves.[29]

The development of the detailed division of labour was a critical part of the more general separation of the intellectual from the corporeal, and of reason from morality. Friedrich Engels observed some decades later that:

> In the division of labour, man is also divided. All other physical and mental faculties are sacrificed to the development of one single activity.[30]

Not only are the faculties of the worker crippled but the removal of the workers from direct relationship to the whole product of their labour meant that the product of labour came to dominate the labourer. Wrote Karl Marx: 'To them, their own social action takes the form of the action of objects, which rule the producers instead of being ruled by them'.[31] People as workers are ruled by their products, and as consumers by consumption goods.

Some of the external forms of dehumanised factory work have begun to be undone in recent decades, and factory work is no longer the dominant form of work in post-industrial societies. But the introduction of the detailed division of labour on a wide scale was part of the fundamental transformation of society and of individuals that the era ushered in. In the eighteenth century economic behaviour became separated from questions of ethics and human values and a parallel separation occurred in the psychological domain of the worker. This separation required a prior separation of mind and the passions, something that Descartes declared.

Humankind has a universal dependence on the natural world for its sustenance. The natural world—considered apart from humankind—provides not only the means of livelihood but the object of our 'life-activity' or 'productive life'. The writings of the early Marx, before he became a Marxist,[32] on alienated work, although largely ignoring the ritual aspects of pre-capitalist work, are still the most penetrating commentaries on the alienating effect of work in industrial society. It might be noted here that the failure of Soviet socialism hinged as much as anything else on its failure to transform the character of work.

Work and leisure are not only divided into distinct activities—temporally and psychologically—but work is seen as what we do to acquire the means to enjoy leisure, where leisure is essentially a period of indolence or of pastimes designed expressly to have no purpose, in other words as 'pass-times'. This is apparent when we consider how it feels to be at work and how it feels to be at home.

> The worker therefore only feels himself outside of his work, and in his work feels outside of himself. He is at home when he is not working, and when he is working he is not at home. His labour is not voluntary but coerced; it is forced labour. It is therefore not the satisfaction of a need [to do fulfilling work]; it is merely a means to satisfy a need external to it. Its alien character emerges clearly in the fact that as soon as no physical or other compulsion exists, labour is shunned like the plague.[33]

The secular Marx could not quite see what is so apparent in these early words; the obverse of the loss of the self in alienated work is the sacred character of unalienated work. Instead of 'sacrificing' themselves to their own lives, in sacred work workers sacrifice themselves to the gods and through this achieve immortality.

This does not mean that work has forever lost its sacred character. Far from it. Nor is this an appeal for a return to some golden age of the nobility of labour. If anything, it is an appeal for a reorganisation of work and a reorientation of our lives so that we all can find greater self-expression in what we do. This is no romantic vision; many people do find work through which they can express themselves, even if it is unpaid work in their homes and backyard workshops. Technological advance holds out marvellous possibilities for spreading the benefits of non-specialisation in work. But it will take some very far-reaching changes in beliefs, including the belief that paid work is the means to a consumption end rather than an expressive activity in itself. Above all it requires the most profound shift in our relationships to the whole, and a recasting of our lives, in order that we may give up doing work for 'selfish' reasons.

1 One notable difference between malls in the West and their Third World counterparts is that there is often a strong police presence in the latter. Admission of the non-consuming poor introduces a shaft of reality that breaks the trance of the middle classes.

2 Richard Wightman Fox and T.J. Jackson Lears (eds), *The Culture of Consumption: Critical Essays in American History, 1880–1980* (Pantheon Books, New York, 1983) p. xii

3 See Stuart Ewen, *All Consuming Images: The Politics of Style in Contemporary Culture* (Basic Books, New York, 1988).

4 Johann Goethe, *Faust*, Part One (Penguin, Harmondsworth, 1949) p. 146

5 Norman O. Brown, *Life Against Death* (Wesleyan University Press, Middletown, Connecticut, 1959) p. 251

6 Ernest Becker, *Escape From Evil* (The Free Press, New York, 1975) p79. Weber expressed the same point less sharply when he wrote that 'money functions as an effective medium of exchange, which is in demand as such, not mere tokens used as purely technical accounting units'—Max Weber, *Economy and Society* (Bedminster Press, New York, 1968) p. 93.

7 Brown, *op. cit.*, p. 245

8 Brown, *op. cit.*, p. 248. This ought to be immediately apparent to the dialectical thinker. 'The secular is the negation of the sacred . . . To understand the secular is to understand its relation to the sacred' (Brown, *op. cit.*, pp. 240 & 242). Secular money has an essentially religious character.

9 Becker, *op. cit.*, pp. 76 & 80

10 Becker, *op. cit.*, pp. 28–29

11 The phrase is from Peter Mathieson, *The Snow Leopard* (Viking Press, New York, 1978) p. 272.

12 Becker, *op. cit.*, p. 31

13 Becker, *op. cit.*, p. 75

14 Becker, *op. cit.*, p. 79

15 Robert Tucker (ed.), *The Marx-Engels Reader* (W.W. Norton & Co., New York, 1972) p. 81. On the conflict between money and religious sentiment, Marx once remarked that the established church would sooner give up 48 of its 49 articles than one forty-ninth of its income.

16 See J.E. Cirlot, *A Dictionary of Symbols* (Routledge, London 1971).

17 '[M]an did not learn to clearly distinguish self from body until quite late in his evolutionary career—in fact he would eventually develop

a severe lesion between self and body, ego and flesh, reason and instinct.' Ken Wilber, *Up From Eden: A Transpersonal View of Human Evolution* (Shambhala, Boston, 1986) p. 42

18 Swami Muktananda, *The Perfect Relationship* (Syda Foundation, South Fallsburg, New York, 1980) p. 59

19 St Mark, viii, 36. In The First Epistle of Paul to Timothy (vi, 10) we read the enormously powerful statement: 'The love of money is the root of all evil'.

20 Goethe, *op. cit.*, p. 91

21 Brown, *op. cit.*, p. 234

22 Brown discusses this at some length, *op. cit.*, pp. 239–252.

23 Mircea Eliade, *The Forge and the Crucible: The Origins and Structures of Alchemy* (Harper and Row, New York, 1971) p. 169. Eliade adds the comment that the alchemists and early metallurgists did not see their work as an activity motivated by the desire to conquer Time or Nature. 'Although he put himself in the place of Time, the alchemist took good care not to assume its role' (*ibid.*, p. 174).

24 Eliade, *ibid.*, pp. 172–73

25 Eliade, *ibid.*, p. 176

26 Eliade, *ibid.*, p. 176

27 What follows is in part stimulated by Harry Braverman's study of the alienation of work, *Labor and Monopoly Capital* (Monthly Review Press, New York 1974) especially Chapter 4.

28 Adam Smith, *Wealth of Nations*, Edwin Cannan Edition (1937) pp. 356, 734–35

29 See Rogers Brubaker, *The Limits to Rationality* (George Allen and Unwin, London, 1984) p. 27

30 Friedrich Engels, *Anti-Duhring* in Tucker, *op. cit.*, pp. 321–22

31 *Capital* in Tucker, *op. cit.*, p. 219

32 Towards the end of his life, surveying the work of his followers, Marx declared 'I am not a Marxist'.

33 Marx, *Economic and Philosophic Manuscripts*, in Tucker, *op. cit.*, p. 60

6 THE SYMBOLIC WORLDVIEW

THE ORIGINS OF RATIONALISM

In Europe before the sixteenth century the dominant world view was organic. People mostly lived in coherent, whole communities in which spiritual and material phenomena were not clearly differentiated. Individual needs were not so much subordinated to those of the community but found expression through those of the community. This is not to deny that these societies were often exploitative and sometimes impoverished, but only to make the point that the way people experienced themselves in the world was radically different from the way we experience ourselves today. The organic view of the world was reflected in people's innermost perceptions of themselves and their relationship with their environment. Morris Berman has written:

> The view of nature which predominated in the West down to the eve of the Scientific Revolution was that of an enchanted world. Rocks, trees, rivers, and clouds were all seen as wondrous, alive, and human beings felt at home in this environment. The cosmos, in short, was a place of *belonging*[1]

The separation of self, with its detached intellect, that came with the European Enlightenment was unimaginable to those who lived a 'participating consciousness', an awareness of self in the world that provided a context for existence. Participating consciousness found expression not only in the daily immersion of ordinary people in the world but in the intellectual products of the age. As we will see, the practice of alchemy, as a way of relating the self to the cosmos, drew its last breaths with the ascendancy of the Scientific Revolution. Alchemy was perhaps the most important intellectual manifestation in European cultures of this mode of awareness. Participating consciousness is the sense within the observing subject that the act of observation is not divorced from the observed object, that the external world is alive and can be known through immediate or unmediated experience in a way different from that due to deliberative reflection. It encompasses the sense that the transformation of the external world is also a transformation of the world within.

So for those possessed of participating consciousness, mind *participates* in the world instead of functioning as a detached organ of perception and cognition. Berman argues that the story of the modern epoch is one of progressive disenchantment and that this disenchantment involved a profound psychological loss. The world apprehended by non-participating consciousness becomes describable in terms of matter and motion, the twin conceptual pillars of the new 'mechanical philosophy'. The philosophy of the Enlightenment, then, was one of disenchantment and non-participation characterised by the rigid separation of the observer and the observed, subject and object. In the new world of modern science, the creativity of paradox was replaced by an intolerance of contradiction; knowledge that could guide us in our daily lives was replaced by facts that could help us calculate. The new way of seeing the world was not confined to the scientific community. The new scientific consciousness that accompanied the new philosophy of the world had the most far-reaching impact on the way we define ourselves and the way we experience ourselves as beings.

Some of the creative elements of the pre/Enlightenment organic worldview are beginning to reemerge in our time, especially in the rise of environmentalism. Much of the inspiration for the philosophy of environmentalism comes from the spiritual outlook of indigenous peoples such as Native Americans and Australian Aborigines. The perception by indigenous people of their relationship to the natural environment has been most influential. When the US Government proposed in 1852 to buy tribal lands, Chief Seattle wrote a powerful statement in response, one that is often quoted.

> Every part of this earth is sacred to my people. Every shining pine needle, every sandy shore, every mist in the dark woods, every meadow, every humming insect. All are holy in the memory and experience of my people. . . . .

This we know: the earth does not belong to man, man belongs to the earth. All things are connected like the blood that unites us all. Man did not weave the web of life, he is merely a strand in it. Whatever he does to the web, he does to himself.[2]

It is apparent that these words express a powerful sense of unity between ourselves and the Earth and that this sense derives from our deepest feelings rather than from a process of analytical thought. But one does not need to go to the life ethic of the New World's indigenous people for this. Chief Seattle's words ring true to people of European origin because they express the truths of the perennial philosophy, the mystical knowledge that has inhered in hundreds of cultures the world over. Many of these cultures have been wholly isolated from each other, which only confirms that the perennial philosophy grows not from ideas that can be transmitted by words but from direct human experience of a shared Universe. Thus in the European tradition we find Chief Seattle's idea expressed precisely by Goethe in two lines from *Faust:*

> And learning to perceive my very brothers
>
> In sky and stream and in the silent glade.[3]

The history of humankind, then, may be divided into two great epochs. The first dates from the emergence of humans and extends up to the time of the European Enlightenment. This vast period was dominated by a symbolic, ritualistic, organic view of nature and the role of humans in it. But the era was not static. A gradual separation of the self-in-here from the world-out-there developed through the period, particularly after the 6th century BC. The self slowly separated from the natural world and began to see itself as an actor acting upon the world. This is the thesis of Ken Wilber in his extraordinary book *Up From Eden: A Transpersonal View of Human Evolution.*

> The self was now separate from the natural world, but seemed *central* to it—and there was its new cosmocentric vision: to be the focal point of the natural world, and to defend this focal self against all odds. The individual created a new and higher substitute self "in here" and a new and higher world "out there"—"higher" because both were, for the first time, differentiated from each other and thus no longer totally fused and confused. Thus there

arose, sometime in the dim past of prehistory, the awakening of a defended self-in-here versus the world-out-there.[4]

While humankind gradually emerged from a state of unconscious fusion with the natural world, it remained magically connected to it. This period witnessed the earliest beginnings of the separate egoic self-sense, a sense of definition that grew and was refined over many centuries. The development of agrarian society was a critical step. But the mass of individuals remained immersed in a community and a consciousness that bespoke a magical relationship with the natural environment and these relationships gave people their identities. Life was a ceremony, a ceremony in which human existence itself could be celebrated because of its inseparability from the whole cosmos. The emergence of the modern separate self robbed life of its essential sacredness.

The Grail legends, among so many mythologies, testify to the fact that the modern malaise of the separation of the self from its original source became the dominant psychological drama many centuries ago. The quest for the Holy Grail describes the trials through which the human soul must go in the journey to recapture the original unity consciousness. That this most fundamental of human urges is recognised by us at some deep level is suggested by the enduring power of the Grail legends through the ages.

The slow separation of the self from the natural world reached a watershed with the onset of the scientific, industrial and political revolutions of the seventeenth and eighteenth centuries in Europe. These marked the beginning of the second great period of human history:

> man did not learn to clearly distinguish self from body until quite late in his evolutionary career—in fact he would eventually develop a severe lesion between self and body, ego and flesh, reason and instinct.[5]

Today, our deepest notions of self-definition, the way we construct ourselves psychologically and the way we carry ourselves through our lives, are shaped by the dramatic changes that the scientific and industrial revolutions ushered in. This is why the way our pre-industrial ancestors apprehended the world around them is incomprehensible to us, and why we in the West have been so ruthlessly dismissive of the ideas and cultures of the original inhabitants of the New World. The technological-industrial revolution and the rise of rationalism destroyed the magic in our lives, and industrial capitalism and its ideologists set out, not wholly unwittingly, to destroy the magic in the lives of native peoples too.

In his history of metallurgy and alchemy, Mircea Eliade has written of the advent of industrial society in the following terms:

> the only revolution comparable to it in the past history of humanity, that is, the discovery of agriculture, provoked upheavals and spiritual breakdowns whose magnitude the modern mind finds it well-nigh impossible to conceive. . . . One must also suppose that the profound spiritual crisis aroused by man's decision *to call a halt and bind himself to the soil,* must have taken many hundreds of years to become completely integrated. . . . The technical discoveries of the modern world, its conquest of Time and Space, represent a revolution of similar proportions, the consequences of which are still very far from having become part of us.[6]

The most profound changes brought about by the triumph of industrial society lay in the deepest parts of human self-definition. There developed a sense of the self as an isolated ego existing inside our bodies, a sense of self in which we as discrete consciousnesses act on the world out there. We came to believe that our daily ways of acting on a dead external world determine our fate so that not the gods but we ourselves could change the world. The scientific-industrial revolution transformed the inner world as much as the outer world. But what was it about the new world of industry, technology and commerce that took people away from participating consciousness and their spiritual identification with Nature?

THE MAKING OF THE INDUSTRIAL EGO

The industrial ego was a product both of dramatic material changes in society and the transformation of the way Europeans construed the world. The birth of industrial capitalism in Europe tore people from their communities and destroyed the age-old patterns of village society, patterns which had integrated the tasks of survival with the flow of household and community life. The flow of life was an unceasing ritual that nurtured the spirit and provided a daily affirmation of a cosmology that bestowed meaning on life. In the new environment the industrial worker became an individual, one whose survival was dependent on the work of the individual and in whom physical reproduction on the one hand and spiritual and social reproduction on the other were split into separate spheres. This was the genesis of modern alienation, the most profound and far-reaching condition afflicting our present society.

The development of wage-labour—the essential social relationship of the new industrial societies—was a truly critical point in the psychological development, as well as the material development, of humankind. In this new social relationship the worker confronted the capitalist as a free individual in the market for labour services. The direct payment of labour for services rendered in the working day was a new form of relationship. In feudal times, and in other modes of production around the world today, economic relationships were and still are infused with social obligation and custom. The spread of the wage-labour relationship thus affected not only 'economic' relationships but all forms of human relationships. In a powerful polemic the contemporary observers Karl Marx and Friedrich Engels wrote:

> The bourgeoisie, wherever it has got the upper hand, has put an end to all feudal, patriarchal, idyllic relations. It has pitilessly torn asunder the motley feudal ties that bound man to his "natural superiors", and has left remaining no other nexus between man and man than naked self-interest, than callous "cash payment". It has drowned the most heavenly ecstasies of religious fervour, of chivalrous enthusiasm, of philistine sentimentalism, in the icy water of egotistical calculation. It has resolved personal worth into exchange value, and in place of the numberless indefeasible chartered freedoms, has set up that single, unconscionable freedom—Free Trade.[7]

Although industrial development saw the rapid growth of towns and cities and threw people physically ever closer, the new urban agglomerations were built on the isolation of the labourer. The nature of urban society was profoundly different—lonely, fractured, and based on the separation of work and trade from family and community. The nature of the family itself began to undergo fundamental changes. The nuclear family emerged, cut off from the wider family now geographically dispersed, dependent on its own resources, with a new intensity of family relationships, in which work and family life were spatially and temporally separated.

Today, large households or communes provide an appropriate form of social living and way of life only for people with a very strong commitment to an ideology or religion. This commitment sets them apart from the normal traffic of everyday social life. For the masses of Western society, atomised households based on nuclear families provide the household structure appropriate to the secular vision.[8] The secular vision entails, above all, a psychological absorption in the economic; it is the economy that provides the guide through life, the framework that lends authority to our thoughts. In the communal household the social community and its sacredness provide the inwardly experienced authority to which members unwittingly turn for guidance.

The nature of work was radically transformed in the new industrial society. While there had always been a social division of labour which allocated people to different trades and occupations, now work was dominated by the detailed division of labour in which each worker performed, repeatedly, the same, often trivial tasks. From a farmer capable of many things, the most important of which was to provide from the farm itself the goods necessary for survival, the worker became crippled by specialisation. The changed nature of work was a crucial part of the transformation of the person into a mere cypher in the marketplace. This was both an objective and a psychological transformation. To echo Eliade's words: 'The secularization of work is like an open wound in the body of modern society.'[9]

With the advent of industrial capitalism, human activity became broken into economic and non-economic activities, a distinction that would have been unfathomable in the household economy. The spread of markets, the division of labour and the growth and privatisation of the means of production were such powerful forces of change that they brought about a fundamental transformation not only in the way in which people sustained themselves physically but also in the way people constructed themselves psychologically.

The emergence of a society of individuals—both objectively as part of the industrial work force and subjectively as people torn from communities—was a critical aspect of the breakdown of European feudalism, a system in which the peasantry were objectively and subjectively slaves, willing servants to the landlords. The emergence of the individual was accompanied by a new set of ideas and legal forms associated with a philosophy of individual rights rather than collective responsibility.

Ironically, the vast social changes that came with the growth of industrial society in Europe can be seen in one sense as the destruction of the possibility of the individual. In the terminology of the great Swiss psychologist Carl Jung, the process of individuation, the formation of a truly free individual, occurs as the material buried in the unconscious mind is progressively made conscious, and the struggle between conscious actions and unconscious motivations disappears. The disintegration of traditional social patterns with the growth of industrial society carried with it the further sundering of the unity of the conscious and the unconscious minds so that a one-sided, distorted development of the personality became the norm.[10]

THE REPRODUCTION OF THE INDUSTRIAL EGO

The production of isolated egos that provide a barrier to psychological participation in the world must be reproduced in each generation. In her remarkable and disturbing book *The Continuum Concept*, Jean Liedloff argues that the pathological character traits of Westerners are reproduced each generation by child-rearing practices that are extraordinarily alienated, that is, divorced from the natural instincts of the human animal.[11] The pervasive and inescapable sense of longing and the loss of a sense of being truly alive are closely related to the deprivation of in-arms experience routinely visited on Western infants. Liedloff contrasts this experience and its consequences for the personality in the West with that of the Yequana Indians who live deep in the rainforests of Venezuela. The absence of neurosis among the Yequana stands in stark contrast to the obsessiveness with which Westerners live their lives. Liedloff shows, by implication, how the profoundly individualistic and alienated concept of self in Western societies is reproduced from generation to generation through our child-rearing practices. While in most societies there appear to have been some people with a strong individualistic inclination, often taking the form of rejection and rebellion, never before have *societies* thought of themselves as agglomerations of individuals. Liedloff shows the capacity for personal misery that this isolation and alienation confers. But the quality of childhood experience does not inevitably consign us to varying degrees of suffering. We must all reach a stage of ego-identification, a stage that is consolidated in the teenage years. The key test is how difficult it is to pass through ego-identification to a higher stage, a stage in which we recognise and identify with the true Self. It is here perhaps, but only perhaps, that a loving childhood confers an advantage.

The evolutionary process of which the scientific-industrial revolution was such a critical watershed is paralleled in the development of the child. As Wilber and others argue, ontogeny recapitulates phylogeny; in broad terms, each individual develops through the stages that humanity itself has traversed. Wilber quotes Piaget on the development of the infant:

> During the early stages the world and the self are one; neither term is distinguished from the other. But when they become distinct, these two terms begin by remaining very close to each other: *the world is still conscious and full of intentions*, the self is . . . only slightly interiorized.[12]

This is a truly remarkable thing to say: the infant does not use reason to prove that the world is dead, but the world appears to lose its consciousness as the child separates from it. Participating consciousness is withdrawn as the infant absorbs the definition of self taught to it by the world. When the infant looks in the mirror, she is told '*That* is you' and the identification sticks, 'I *am* my image in the mirror, the face I present to the world'.

Many have commented on the fact that the transition from medieval society was accompanied by changes in child-rearing practices. Berman notes in particular the changes in ideas and practices regarding body contact and the psychological implications of separation and dissociation.[13] The most profound differences in psychological development are explained by Liedloff by the quantity and quality of in-arms experience. These ideas and practices defined the notion of childhood itself. Prior to the end of the sixteenth century neither the nuclear family nor the child existed as concepts. The seventeenth century literally 'discovered' childhood.

As a result of the massive social dislocation brought about by the emergence of industrial society—the fracturing of communities, the diaspora of workers, the growth of individualised work, the transformation of the family, the rapidity of change—people became isolated from local society yet more dependent on the larger society. We have become objective individuals, for that is how society constructs us; but subjectively we are enslaved. In our society individuals are not true individuals. We claim freedom in our politics and we claim freedom for ourselves in our daily lives. Yet our important decisions afford no choice at all; the decision is already made by our social conditioning. But just as those who do not truly believe are the most fanatical devotees, so we cling desperately to the illusion of freedom.

The psychology of non-participation and the self-definition it reflects are reproduced and reinforced every day. We are bombarded by the ideology of science, the notion that all is knowable, that human development is a process of progressive discovery of a finitely knowable universe. Every time we learn of a new discovery it suggests that a bit more of the unknown becomes known to us and is thereby conquered. We have even begun to unlock the mysteries of space, conquering it with space travel, extending the physical boundaries of the known, as though by looking ever further outward we can avoid the anguish of looking inward. This science of knowing is a science of control; our egos fear the unknown because it is outside of us and therefore a threat. Science serves, then, as a false unification of the subject and object, the fundamental duality that defines our character. We sit back as detached observers of the universe, analysers who think about the world outside us. Our non-participation in the world is doubly reinforced by the activities that dominate our societies—work whose aim is to put objects into the market, and recreation. Watching television is the ultimate act of non-participation. The world is taken away, shaped and moulded, packaged and made 'more exciting' and then served up behind a glass screen.

For some, it would seem, the cycle of reproduction continues until one day something breaks through—some glimmer, or explosion, of understanding that there are no boundaries, that we are one. A secret creeps into their minds, a secret that changes them forever, the deepest knowledge that cannot be pushed back down for long, a truth that can only grow. This is an age-old transformation that the rituals of the past deliberately tried to induce.

> But then, perhaps, on occasion, in the precincts of the temple, dancing ground, or some sacred site, the fleeting wisp of a sense of some mystery beyond, in the face of which all of this is trivial nonsense, may be experienced and therein . . . [an] amplification of the individual's horizon of experience and depth of realization through his spiritual death and resurrection . . . [14]

In a curious book written in the 1890s and entitled *Cosmic Consciousness,* an American physician named Richard Bucke details the 'cosmic' experiences of fifty Westerners ranging from the unknown to the famous.[15] The latter include Francis Bacon, Dante, Walt Whitman, Spinoza and Wordsworth. Sometimes when we read the works of these people we have a sense that they have seen something deeper, something that is perhaps in all of us but just beyond our grasp.

THE NEW EGO AND THE NEW ECONOMICS

The far-reaching psychological changes brought about by the scientific-industrial revolution cannot be separated from another vital component of that period of revolutionary change in Europe—the revolution in social structures on which the new economics was built.

Two hundred years before the era of mass consumer culture, the psychology and the programme of the new middle classes and their thinkers was to capture the world by force of reason and science. Berman puts it elegantly:

> For the middle and upper classes, at least, the vacuum left by the Protestant attack on the supernatural could be filled by prayer and worldly success. . . . Throughout Northern Europe, both the notion of secular salvation and the mechanical philosophy informed the world view of the rising bourgeoisie; it was their spiritual needs alone that would be catered to. . . . The Puritan values of competitiveness, orderliness, and self-control came to typify a world that had previously regarded such behavior as aberrant . . . . For what was ultimately created by the shift from animism to mechanism was not merely a new

science, but a new personality to go with it; and Isaac Newton can rightly be seen as a microcosm, or epitome, of these changes.[16]

When the new bourgeoisie looked in the mirror for the first time it found *homo economicus*, rational economic man. The economists took their cue and began to build a new science of society on this reflected self. For their part, the new proletariat and the remnants of the peasantry attempted to cling to the old but doomed organic view with its magic and alchemical notions of the spirit in matter that joined humans with the whole natural world. Like so much of the change of the time, the attack by science and Protestantism on the old ways took on the character of a class struggle. Writes Berman of the popular alchemical vision of the world: 'During this period, then, Hermeticism had an unmistakable socialist edge'.[17]

The new science not only served as the basis for technological development but, as we will see in the discussion of alchemy, provided the essential rationale for the reconceptualisation of Nature, its division into a catalogue of resources whose values arise not from direct appreciation of Nature but from the possibility of exploiting it. The Earth was by this act murdered; it was natural, then, to dissect it. For the new bourgeoisie:

> Not only was the idea of living matter heresy to such groups; it was also economically inconvenient. A dead earth ruptures the delicate ecological balance that was maintained in the alchemical tradition, but if nature is dead, there are no restraints on exploiting it for profit. Loving cultivation becomes rape ... [18]

Economics accurately mirrored the emergence of the objective individual—the conceptual framework of the industrial ego—and its relationship to the 'factors of production' that now surrounded it. To be fully separate from the natural world and to refuse to participate in it became a necessary component of sanity.

Sanity became inseparable from a specific form of rationality. The rationality of economics is thus in no sense timeless and universal. This was very much the argument of the early sociologist Max Weber.[19] Weber argued that the essence of modern capitalism is its rationality. Market exchange, which along with wage labour are the pillars of capitalism, is of its essence rational, in the sense that all commitments other than pure economic self-interest are irrelevant. Moreover, all moral claims, family and clan loyalties, rites, obligations and social traditions are stripped away. In previous eras, the act of exchange was filled with social as well as economic significance. The economics of traditional societies lies largely in systems of gift exchange. Discussing Weber, Rogers Brubaker writes:

> The market is the paradigm of rationality in this double sense, for market exchange, more than any other type of activity, is determined by the deliberate and calculating pursuit of self-interest and is free from the multifarious fetters of tradition and the capricious influence of feelings.[20]

In other words, the marketplace is intensely impersonal, a place where actions are motivated by self-interested calculation among distinct individuals. It permits the full expression of instrumentalist desire. The use of advanced forms of monetary measurement and monetary exchange permit the depersonalisation of market transactions and the dominance of instrumental calculation. Rather than weighing up a range of implications from an exchange—financial implications, social obligations, considerations of caste and class—free individuals in the market can measure the consequences of their actions by one parameter, the monetary balance to be had from the exchange. Wrote Weber:

> From a purely technical point of view, money is the most 'perfect' means of economic calculation. That is, it is formally the most rational means of orienting economic activity. Calculation in terms of money is thus the specific means of rational economic provision.[21]

Just as fundamental to the rationality of exchange is the rationality of production under capitalism. The production process—from Adam Smith's pin factory to the 'scientific management' of Taylorism—began under capitalism to be organised solely with the goal of rational calculation of the maximum value of output derivable from the available inputs. These inputs included, most critically of all, wage labour, that is, labour employed at a fixed wage to perform predetermined duties within the enterprise. This was a very new relationship, peculiar to capitalism. Human labour, perhaps the most fundamental expression of human nature, became a mere component of factory production, one whose cost could be minimised, whose effort could be measured, whose non-economic consequences could be disregarded, and whose services could be terminated when the calculations decreed.

The rationality of our economic world, therefore, is peculiar to the economic system that emerged with the scientific-industrial revolution. The dominance of rationality has seen a psychological shift of truly historic importance, one with few precedents in the history of humankind. The most important of our daily activities lost their sacred character; as a result, our inner worlds were further banished from our conscious minds and trivialised to the point where most of us feel ashamed to discuss our inner worlds publicly or even to acknowledge them to ourselves. This is not to decry the value of rationality as such, but to recognise its specific form in Western society and, above all, to point to its crippling effects when it is allowed to dominate all else.

THE NEW MACHINE WORLD

In the sixteenth and seventeenth centuries the medieval outlook, which was still imbued with much of the spirit of the perennial philosophy, changed radically. The organic world view was replaced by a view of the world as a machine. The world became divided into two distinct parts—the part comprised of humans, and the rest, a giant machine controllable by humans. René Descartes was a major force in the transition to this new way of thinking about the world, this age of the Scientific Revolution. In the words of Fritjof Capra:

> Descartes' method is analytic. It consists in breaking up thoughts and problems into pieces and in arranging these in their logical order. . . . This analytic method of reasoning . . . has become an essential characteristic of modern scientific thought and has proved extremely useful in the development of scientific theories and the realization of complex technological projects.[22]

In the seventeenth century, Newton developed a complete mathematical formulation of the mechanical view of nature. For the first time the world was described by a set of mutually consistent relationships that lent themselves to rational disproof. These posed the most profound challenge to primordial ideas about the cosmos and the place of humans in it. A few central scientific concepts were used to build a systematic explanation of the observable phenomena of the earth and the cosmos. Religious dogmas could not withstand the withering force of scientific reason—particularly when the latter was in the service of such an overwhelmingly powerful social force as industrial wealth—and as religion came crashing down so did our certainties about our cosmic significance, the ideas that gave human existence a sense of solidity, permanence and purpose. The Newtonian universe was one huge mechanical system, operating according to exact mathematical laws, laws comprehensible only to a select few.[23] It was a system that could be used devastatingly to ridicule the pre-scientific beliefs of those resistant to change; but it could not provide the new believers in reason with a replacement set of ideas that could afford comfort through life's vicissitudes. The triumph of rationalism, then, had a profound impact on how people as psychological beings were constructed.

Newton introduced the proper mixture of the empirical, inductive scientific method and the rational, deductive method and his system of ideas was an essential foundation of the fantastic expansion of productive power that characterised the Industrial Revolution and the modern economic systems of the Western industrialised world to which it gave rise. Here was the substitute for the cosmological certainties of religion; the purpose of life became material progress.

The method of reductionism—'the belief that all aspects of complex phenomena can be understood by reducing them to their constituent parts'[24]—is fundamental to economics. Economic method replicates the nineteenth century reductionist method of science, the still-dominant mode of official thought in the West. This does not mean that there are not economic systems that attempt to capture the workings of the machine as a whole. The systems of renowned economists Leon Walras and Arrow and Debreu do this. The reductionist method does mean, however, that the working of the machine as a whole is seen as the interaction of the myriad component parts. The machine always remains the sum of its parts; there is no knowledge to be had from looking into its essence rather than its form, from direct appreciation of its nature rather than analysis of its workings.

Moreover, the economic way of constructing the individual owes a great deal to the rigid Cartesian division between mind and matter. Descartes wrote that 'there is nothing included in the concept of body that belongs to the mind; and nothing in that of mind that belongs to the body'. Capra comments thus:

> The Cartesian division between mind and matter has . . . taught us to be aware of ourselves as isolated egos existing 'inside' our bodies . . . [25]

This was a truly radical idea, one that was a great step towards the modern mode of self-awareness. It was also a great step towards the alienation of our conscious minds from our true natures and the sundering of our essential relationship with the natural world, our nurturing environment.

> This inner fragmentation mirrors our view of the world 'outside' which is seen as a multitude of separate objects and events. The natural environment is treated as if it consisted of separate parts to be exploited by different interest groups.[26]

The material progress of the scientific-industrial revolution was built on the idea of calculability. Max Weber stressed the extraordinary importance of calculability as the basis for efficient capital accounting and thus profit making.[27] Rational decision making depends wholly on the ability to calculate outcomes. There is no place for intuition. Calculation excludes those factors, the moral and religious factors, that do not lend themselves to the calculus. 'In the market economy every form of rational calculation . . . is oriented to expectations of prices and their changes.'[28] The need for certainty and predictability becomes all-embracing psychologically as well as commercially. It is here that we find the roots of our obsession with knowing the future, with the dominance of left-brain functions.

The relationship between the Newtonian physical system and modern economics is more direct than the industrial opportunities afforded by scientific developments. The corpus of economic ideas that now dominates our world grew directly out of the Newtonian-Cartesian worldview. In the Newtonian world, all physical phenomena took place in a three dimensional space. All changes occurred in a separate dimension called time which flows smoothly from the past through the present to the future.[29]

> The mechanistic view of nature is thus closely related to a rigorous determinism. The giant cosmic machine was seen

as being completely causal and determinate. All that happened had a definite cause and gave rise to a definite effect, and the future of any part of the system could—in principle—be predicted with absolute certainty if its state at any time was known in all details.[30]

This idea of a deterministic system was lifted from classical physics and applied verbatim to economic systems. It seemed natural for the economists of the nineteenth century, immersed in the Lockean world of social theory, to apply these apparently scientific conceptions to the economic aspect of society. Once certain initial conditions are known it is possible in principle to predict precisely how an economy will evolve. There are only two constraints to perfect foresight—incomplete progress towards the correct theory of how the system works, and practical limitations on the amount of data that would need to be collected and the computing power of the calculating machine.

The Newtonian view of the physical universe had a powerful impact on all areas of thought in the eighteenth and nineteenth centuries. It swept away old magical, pre-rational notions and replaced them with more powerful ideas. It was applied to the analysis of society by John Locke in particular. Locke developed a theory of society in which people entered as atoms into the whole. With the whole made up of its atoms, society could then be understood by examining the behaviour of the atoms and their interaction. This was a radically new idea in its generality. Indeed, the notion of society itself, as a collectivity of individuals, was new. The notion of an *individual,* an independent, free-standing being, was the essential philosophical foundation for such far-reaching new ideas as human rights, private property and political democracy.

The revolutionary ideas of the Enlightenment served well the purpose of breaking down European feudalism which was not only exploitative but was holding back the thrusting power of the productive forces being unleashed by technological discoveries and the growth of towns. These enormous social and economic changes found philosophical expression in utilitarianism. In its early years, utilitarianism was a political and social as well as an economic doctrine. Known also as Philosophical Radicalism, in later years it provided the intellectual foundation for fundamental reforms in English legal and political institutions in the nineteenth century. While these new ideas and social forces swept away the old order based on the obligations of feudal society, utilitarianism cannot, as it implicitly claims to do, sweep away social relations as such. In fact there is a sort of naive idealism in the idea that prior to the triumph of market capitalism economic and other decisions were governed by irrational, feudal obligations and the imperatives of a rigidly hierarchical social order, while all that drives decision-making under market capitalism are the free, rational choices of individuals deciding how to spend their money and allocate their resources. If *homo economicus* is a universal model of human behaviour in all societies and for all types of behaviour (after Gary Becker), then it must also be able to explain feudalism itself.

The economists' reply could perhaps be along the lines that, under feudalism, *noblesse oblige* and the tithe formed components of the economic agents' (that is, the serfs' and landlords') objective functions so that the feudal outcome merely expressed the preferences of all agents. For peasants, paying the tithe to the landlord was then a means of satisfying the 'objective function' of the peasant, a function which incorporated the desire to satisfy social obligations to the landlord. It is apparent from this what a deeply conservative ideology underlies modern economics. The ideas of neoclassical economic analysis could be applied to justify feudalism itself, the mode of social organisation which capitalism had to destroy in order to flourish.

In the world of science, the Newtonian system came under severe challenge towards the end of the nineteenth century and especially in the 1920s. It is now recognised as only an approximation (albeit a very good one) under certain physical conditions. It cannot, however, answer some of the most important questions. Physics broke matter down into finer and finer components until it became apparent that there was no absolute, immutable speck of matter that formed the building block of every thing. New explanations had to emerge—explanations in which matter and energy became equivalent, where light is sometimes a particle and sometimes a wave, where space and time merge, where space can be curved and time is no longer linear, where the object of study is no longer independent of the person observing it.[31]

Modern economics could never follow the physicists' path to 'enlightenment' and the Newtonian method continues to drive economics in its attempt to deprive human actors of their essential aliveness by classifying their economic behaviour according to a set of well-defined rules. The model of behaviour that economics imposes on humans reflects an aspect of the reality that people face in their daily lives and to that extent it has been responsible for some important insights into human behaviour. But its partial character has led it to some highly distorted perceptions and some very destructive policy conclusions.

ALCHEMY AND THE SYMBOLIC WORLDVIEW

The trivialisation of the inner world that so characterises our society was not always so, even among the foundation thinkers of the philosophical revolution. As we will see, even a scientist as seminal as Newton acknowledged, albeit privately, the validity of the inner world. Perhaps the most explicit integration in science of the roles of mystic and savant occurs in the history of alchemy. To the modern mind, alchemy appears to run directly contrary to the truths of twentieth-century science, and is no more than a historical curiosity. But a proper understanding of the alchemical opus can teach us a great deal about our selves, our work and our world.

At one level, alchemy was the practice of attempting to turn base metals into gold or to distil the elixir of life through the processes of chemical transformation. But it went a great deal deeper. There were independent alchemical traditions in Greece, Arabia, India and China as well as in Europe. Alchemy reached its heyday towards the end of the sixteenth and the seventeenth century but was still widely practiced in the eighteenth century. It would be difficult to explain the persistence of alchemy over many centuries and in several major civilisations if it were no more than a naive and greedy attempt to do the physically impossible. In fact, running in parallel to the physical processes, at a deeper level, a level at which the wiser alchemists consciously operated, the work was aimed at a psychic or spiritual transformation. The goal was philosopher's gold, *aurum philosophicum*. Repeatedly they declared: 'Our gold is not the common gold'. The transformation they pursued was not the outer transformation of base metals into gold but of the psyche; the quest was for the extraction of purity of spirit or knowledge of one's Self. For them, writes one commentator, alchemy was

> an unconscious psychological experiment for the perfection of their own internal being. That is, the liberation of the 'gold' within themselves as personified and explicated in the liberation of gold from matter.[32]

Many practitioners of the art were undoubtedly convinced at a conscious level that their goal was nothing more than the physical transformation of chemicals. Some, known as 'puffers', were charlatans who sought to profit from superstition. In this century, Carl Jung rediscovered the deeper purpose of alchemy, a purpose whose relevance is as vital as ever.

> But there were always a few for whom laboratory work was primarily a matter of symbols and their psychic effect. As the texts show, they were quite conscious of this, to the point of condemning the naive gold-makers as liars, frauds, and dupes. Their own standpoint they proclaimed with propositions like "Aurum nostrum non est aurum vulgi." Although their labours over the retort were a serious effort to elicit the secrets of chemical transformation, it was at the same time—and often in overwhelming degree—the reflection of a parallel psychic process which could be projected all the more easily into the unknown chemistry of matter since that process is an unconscious phenomenon of nature, just like the mysterious alteration of substances.[33]

Another commentator, Mircea Eliade, makes the same observation with respect to the first stage of the alchemical process, the reduction of the substance to its basic matter, in preparation for a psychological rebirth.

> The *materia prima* should not be understood merely as a primordial condition of the substance but also as an inner experience of the alchemist. The reduction of matter to its original condition of absolute indifferentiation, corresponds, on the plane of inner experience, to the regression to the pre-natal, embryonic state.[34]

The path to spiritual wholeness has taken many forms, from explicitly religious practices such as identification with god or an embodiment of god (the guru), prayer, ritual arts such as tai chi, asceticism, and especially meditation in all its forms. For the alchemists, their spiritual practice was the ritual work of transformation of physical substances. For the more sophisticated alchemists their work was a conscious devotional activity. Their eyes were firmly on Atman, the godhead. It is a nice irony that their work lends itself so easily to misinterpretation as the modern substitute for god—the accumulation of gold. For whatever personal reasons, the alchemists began with an understanding of the veil-like nature of the ego and were willing to confront ego-death. The product of the serious alchemical opus was transcendence, that subtle but all-powerful knowledge: 'This "wisdom" reserved exclusively for those who have anticipated the experience of death at the height of life'.[35]

The philosophy of alchemy stood in direct contrast to the most important new ideas of the Scientific Revolution, in particular the separation of the observer and the observed. In Berman's words:

> The "Hermetic wisdom", as it has been called, was in effect dedicated to the notion that real knowledge occurred only via the union of subject and object .... With the Scientific Revolution, the considerable remnants of original participation were finally ousted, and this process constituted a significant episode in the history of Western consciousness.[36]

The objectivity that marked the scientific outlook of the Enlightenment contradicted the 'participating consciousness' of alchemy, and indeed, the everyday appreciation of the world by the mass of ordinary people in all of their activities. For those who live in them, these two worlds—objective, scientific, ego-identifying consciousness and participating, numinous consciousness—are mutually incomprehensible.

Both alchemy and modern industrial science seek to change the material world, to interfere with the processes of Nature. The alchemists, like the metallurgists and other crafts people of the earth, were always aware of the sacredness of their task, for they sought to augment or hasten God's work. They sought permission from Nature through ritual and humility. The correct attitude was one of working in harmony with the Earth, to cooperate with natural processes, rather than to work against Nature, to dominate, to exploit and to master. Indeed, they saw only Nature working with Nature. All of that changed with the coming of science, industry and the Enlightenment in the sixteenth and seventeenth centuries. Then,

> the sacred and the manipulative were split down the middle. The latter could easily survive in a context of profit, expanding technology, and secular salvation. . . . [T]he domination of nature always lurked as a possibility within the Hermetic tradition, but was not seen as separable from its esoteric framework until the Renaissance.[37]

But the inner struggle between the sacred and the profane has been carried on within modern science. Even the most important founding thinker of the new secular science was as much mystic as savant. Isaac Newton himself, locked away in his rooms at Cambridge, devoted twenty years of his life to the study of alchemy, some of this time while he was writing his *Principia Mathematica*. Newton, the father of the Scientific Revolution, the man who invented the analytic method, was a clandestine alchemist. Indeed, he has been called alchemy's 'last great practitioner' and 'regarded himself as the inheritor of an archaic tradition' with a special responsibility to keep it alive.[38] Throughout his life he maintained an intense interest in the occult.

Newton was cleaned up for public view by his rationalist admirers in the eighteenth century. Newton himself, recognising the confusion and disillusion that would flow from public knowledge that the great separator of subject and object himself immersed his own soul into the material world, was discrete about his hermetic activities and beliefs.[39] Nevertheless, he had a large alchemical library and his alchemical experiments were an inseparable feature of his life at least until he was appointed Master of the Mint in 1696 at the age of 54. One commentator has argued that alchemy was Newton's 'most enduring passion, and the *Principia* something of an interruption of this larger quest.'[40]

Newton's alchemical endeavours were a last vestige of a previous age. The Scientific Revolution and the Enlightenment spawned a new and radically different era, one that has invested our own thinking with such a fundamentally different quality that we find older modes of thought utterly mysterious. But in the very deepest reaches of our minds we still understand. The knowledge of archaic societies—of ritual, of sacredness, of sacrifice—cannot be expunged by any amount of reason and indeed cannot help but impose itself on the unbeliever in strange and disturbing way.

Why, it might be asked, was the European spiritual quest traced out through the medium of alchemy? What was the connection between the experimental practices of the 'spagyric art' and the goal of spiritual transformation? The link lies in the power of symbols, a power that persists beyond the demise of alchemy. Symbols are manifest representations or triggers of the deepest states of being; they can induce emotional responses or states of awareness beyond emotion which go directly to the nature of being.

The power of symbols resides in their ability to penetrate deeper than the cogitations of the rational mind, to strike at the centre of our intuitive understanding, the mind in the heart. The principal function of a living mythological symbol is to stimulate inner life energies—deep responses to images of growth, birth, unity, sustenance, wisdom, courage, conflict and death. Wrote Jung:

> In psychotherapy it often happens that, long before they reach consciousness, certain unconscious tendencies betray their presence by symbols, occurring mostly in dreams but also in waking fantasies and symbolic actions.[41]

In the symbolic world, the normal laws of logic are not relevant yet there is coherence and meaning aplenty. As an illustration, dreams often have a coherence, a sense of consistency, but they are not logical in the usual way. Dreams do not lose their meaning by their lack of formal logic. In this inner world, power resides in symbols rather than facts. It is a world within all of us and one which influences our every action and thought.

These outer and inner worlds are not really separate, but are two aspects of the same thing. We see one side or the other depending on how we perceive things. The familiar optical illusion of the candlestick-cum-two faces is a good way of thinking about it. Imagine that you had never seen a candlestick or anything like it. It would be impossible to recognise that aspect of the object. In the era since the European Enlightenment we have largely suppressed our ability to recognise the inner, symbolic form of things. We have suppressed our ability to see into the qualitative nature of things. This very much changes our conscious relationship with those things, that is, how we feel about them, and in particular, how we *value* them. In the outside world, when separated from the inside world, the natural environment becomes a 'resource' and its values are economic.

It is also true, however, that our ability to see the 'dual' nature of things is inherent in us as humans and we have only pushed our qualitative awareness into our unconscious minds. Our unconscious minds have a very powerful, and often acutely uncomfortable, influence over our thoughts and our actions. The symbolic significance of things is not lost on our unconscious minds. Using our example, if for some reason I had repressed the image of the candlestick because my father had beaten me with one, I would probably have all of the feelings of recognising it without the conscious thought. On the other hand, if I had never seen a candlestick I would find the beliefs of those who could see it incomprehensible. I could attempt to prove rationally that there was no candlestick there, only the faces, but it would convince only those others who could not recognise it. The reality of the inner world is crushingly obvious to those who see it. The enormous emphasis that our society places on scientific understanding and on the ability of one person or group to *prove* things to others has been a critical aspect to our lost ability to see and understand the numinous, symbolic world that surrounds and absorbs us.

Symbols go directly, but often unconsciously, to the basic patterns of our psyches. They cannot be understood by rational analysis and codification, they can only be experienced, as Goethe knew:

No dusty logic can divine
The meaning of a sacred sign.[42]

Today we have mostly lost the conscious appreciation of the power and importance of symbols. But since these symbols are inseparable from human life experience they have simply gone underground and drive our lives, as it were, from the back seat. To the extent that our world is constructed on the ground of conscious ideas that are at variance with our inner drives, the psychological outcome is entirely different.

> . . . a thinking dominated by cosmological symbolism created an experience of the world vastly different from that accessible to modern man. To symbolic thinking the world is not only 'alive' but also 'open': an object is never simply itself (as is the case with modern consciousness), it is also a sign of, or a repository for, something else.[43]

The alchemical opus appears a great deal more understandable when we recognise the fundamentally different conception of the relationship between the person and the surrounding world that the participating consciousness lived. We can begin to appreciate why the alchemists pursued their task through chemical experiments. Then, the modern rigid distinction between the experimenter and the materials of the world on which the experiments were carried out was no barrier. When they could unite themselves with the materials with which they worked the alchemists who transformed the outside world were, *ipso facto*, transforming themselves.

This process is apparent from the symbolic content of some of the most important procedures of alchemy. In alchemy, gold symbolised the final state of union, the Holy Grail, the goal of spiritual practice. The chemical reactions themselves were symbols of psychological transformation. The phases of chemical transformation—the *nigredo*, the *albedo*, the *rubedo*—symbolised the phases of psychic growth, closely mirrored in Jung's idea of individuation, the process of maturity to wholeness which today is sometimes referred to and trivialised as the mid-life crisis.

We have already seen that the first stage of the alchemical opus, reduction to the *prima materia*, symbolises the return to the embryonic state in preparation for rebirth. The chemical reactions that took place in the alembic were symbols of psychological or spiritual transformation. *Purification*, the repeated dissolution of the material and burning off of impurities, symbolises the difficult process of transcending the limits of ego in search of the true self. The *nigredo*, an early stage of the opus, is the blackening of the chemical material, the darkening or putrefaction, and symbolises the despair, the depression and the suffering that is the first phase of the spiritual transformation. And of course *gold*, the final goal of the labours of the laboratory, is the distillation of the essence of matter, in all of its purity, the true Self of divine creation; this can only be the attainment of spiritual purity, liberation from the dross of life, the gold within.[44]

For the alchemists, the symbolism of their experiments was the essence of the art, although they themselves did not draw the sharp latterday distinction between the thing itself and its symbolic significance or power in the world. For one immersed in a symbolic world view there is no symbolism.

The triumph of the Enlightenment was the defeat of the symbolic worldview. Scientific progress saw the death of the living Universe and the birth of an impersonal cosmology outside of our selves. The penetration of the Universe by rational human thought robbed it of its sacred character. For all of its wondrous inventions, this was the curse of Science. Lame Deer, a Lakota medicine man, tried to grasp the difference between the Native American way of being and that of the white invaders. All things are sacred.

> We Indians live in a world of symbols and images where the spiritual and the commonplace are one. To you symbols are just words, spoken or written in a book. To us they are part of nature, part of ourselves—the earth, the sun, the wind and the rain, stones, trees, animals, even the little insects like ants and grasshoppers. We try to understand them not with the head but with the heart, and we need no more than a hint to give us the meaning.

THE WAY OF KNOWING

It is ironical that the term 'Enlightenment' is used to describe a period that witnessed the triumph of reason at the expense of the suppression of the inner world. In the Eastern mystical tradition, in Buddhist and Hindu thought, enlightenment refers to the process of gaining deeper awareness of the inner world. This pursuit of knowledge of our psyches, of the forces that truly drive us, is also the way to personal development in some formal psychologies in the West, those of Jung and Maslow, as well as of the informal 'personal growth' movement. From the original perspective of the European Enlightenment, pursuit of the inner self would appear to be regression to a dark and primitive pre-Enlightenment era, whereas in reality it represents a movement beyond the fixation with ego, exclusive rationality and the material world. The movement beyond rationality in no sense rejects the power of reason but, recognising the limits that exclusive focus on the world of rationality places on our development, incorporates reason in a broader world of experience and understanding.

The formal search for natural explanations and rational causes perhaps began with the Pythagoreans in the sixth century BC. The Pythagorean school was responsible not only for great advances in mathematics but for the elevation of mathematics to a position of reverence in the realm of human experience. The celebration of mathematics by the Pythagoreans was not accompanied by a purging of the world of its mystical quality. Quite the reverse; explication of the domain of mathematical reason was seen as a means to deeper insight into, and glorification of, the world of spiritual awareness. Wrote Koestler, for the Pythagoreans,

> by relating music to astronomy and both to mathematics, emotional experience became enriched and deepened by intellectual insight. Cosmic wonder and aesthetic delight no longer live apart from the exercise of reason; they are all inter-related. . . . They were aware that the symbols of mythology and the symbols of mathematical science were different aspects of the same, indivisible Reality. . . . It is a state of mind very difficult for twentieth century man to imagine . . . [45]

Indeed, Koestler characterises the process of scientific development, at least up to the time of the Enlightenment, as the union of the mystic and the savant.

> The mystic and the savant jointly satisfied the dual urge of allaying the self's cosmic anxiety and of transcending its limitations; its dual needs for protection and liberation . . . . It is therefore a perverse mistake to identify the religious need solely with intuition and emotion, science solely with the logical and the rational. . . . In the history of the race, as of the individual, both branches of the

cosmic quest originate in the same source. The priests were the first astronomers; the medicine-men were both prophets and physicians; the techniques of hunting, fishing, sowing and reasoning were imbued with religious magic and ritual.[46]

This sort of awareness still remains in some scientists. The elation at solving a theorem or a scientific problem sometimes goes beyond a feeling of accomplishment—a product of the ego. Sometimes there is a feeling of awe at the *sheer beauty* of the solution, something quite divorced from the intellectual input of the thinker.[47] Scientists like Kepler, Leibniz and Boyle were deeply religious thinkers. Some refused to put their scientific work and their religious convictions into separate compartments. The world, however, would acknowledge only their science.

We have argued that in more recent centuries there has been a new estrangement between the religious and the physical worlds, the inner and the outer worlds. This estrangement saw the gradual victory of 'reason' over 'religion' in the eighteenth and nineteenth centuries, to the point where scientists, the embodiment of the powers of reason, were elevated to the position of saviours of the human race, a role previously reserved for the guardians of the spiritual world. A new humility has been demanded by developments in the physical sciences—as the contradictions between our rationalist methods of cognition and the subtleties and complexities of the world in which we live enforce a reconsideration of the power of traditional scientific reason to reveal all of the mysteries of the universe. But no such doubts have been raised in the economics profession. It is still as firmly as ever, in fact more than ever, convinced that the problems of economic systems and the advancement of human welfare—even though those economies are created by people—can be solved solely by the application of more rational analysis of the material world around us.

The division between an outer reality and a numinous inner world was unquestionably one of the most far-reaching philosophical transitions of human history. It has fundamentally changed the way we think about ourselves and our place on the Earth. In some vital ways the transition was liberating. It enabled the objective world to be seen and understood with a clarity hitherto impossible. It banished irrational, magical, primitive beliefs from the material world of production and commerce, beliefs which had restrained the understanding of the physical world and its technological potential. The liberating ideas of the Enlightenment permitted the fantastic material benefits of the technological-industrial revolution in Europe which, in a brief 200 years, has transformed our outer worlds in ways truly unimaginable.

The tragedy is that the flourishing of our outer worlds has been accompanied by the absolute impoverishment of our inner worlds. While the separation of the objective and subjective worlds has seen the triumph of reason, it has also witnessed the denigration and trivialisation of our subjective reality. The distinction has gone beyond one simply of facilitating analytical processes applied to the material environment; it is one in which the objective world has been elevated to the plane of absolute truth, a jealous god to be worshipped, while the subjective world, our inner reality, is dismissed as inferior, unscientific and, above all, irrational. We do not learn to recognise, develop and trust our inner worlds but to focus on the outer reality by striving for material riches and socially accepted forms of success. Indeed, we are even told that our inner worlds do not really exist, that they are merely products of our imaginations, although nowhere is the source of our imaginations explained.

The express purpose of the building of economic models, and of economics itself, is to describe the world, to capture its functioning and to predict its next moves. This is so deeply inherent in the act of economic analysis that it never bears comment. Yet it is a direct product of the worldview of the Newtonian scientific revolution. The modern Western view of knowledge, which derives from Plato, insists that knowing begins by separating the knower from the object of knowledge. The separate subject learns about the object through observation. The knower does no more than uncover the knowledge for it exists independently of the knower. As we have seen, Berman characterises the new attitude to knowledge that came with the Enlightenment as 'non-participating consciousness'.[48] This is to be distinguished from participating consciousness, which characterises some other (especially traditional) cultures, those that retain a symbolic view of the world. To the latter type of 'mind', Newtonian science and its concept of causality can only describe one aspect of the world. Indeed, the concept of knowing has radically changed as a result of the rigid subject-object dualism. Prior to the Enlightenment, 'to know' meant to enter into, to apprehend in the act of identification with. Dissolution of subject and object meant that to know something was to experience it—an act which, for all the spiritual ravages of the Enlightenment, we rely on constantly in our daily lives, even if we deny it in our conscious calculations. The Biblical use of the word 'know' (which survives in the expression 'carnal knowledge') expressed the identity of the sensual and the intellectual, of idea of *mystical union*.[49] The dissolution of the self in the sexual act (*le petit mort*) is one of the most powerful everyday manifestations of participating consciousness and explains why some spiritual traditions celebrate sexual union. But the splitting of the intellect from the viscera has changed the definition and the experience of knowledge. The language of rationality is the language of intellectual knowledge and it serves in a thousand subtle ways to distance us from the thing, to deny the knowledge of intuition, of identification, of unmediated apprehension, the knowledge that does not describe, codify and control but which gives rise to radical insight into the nature of things. Intellectual knowledge, by denying the validity of participating knowledge, has meant for us a decline in our understanding of the world.

The idea that the world is ultimately knowable, that discovering the whole truth is only a matter of more scientific investigation, fulfils a critical psychological function in Western industrial society. The association between 'knowing' a thing and controlling it means that our urge to control our physical and social environment is advanced above all by understanding its laws and being able to predict their paths. The need to know has become neurosis, for ignorance is feared as failure, as confusion, as inability to control.

The need to know is inseparable from the intellectualisation of our world, the destruction of its magic by means of rationality. Because we believe that in principle everything can be known and explained—by us, as separate knowers—we have purged our world of mystery.

There is no mystery in a machine-universe. The concept of

> "mystery" itself is reduced to the level of an "unsolved problem". Mystery as the dark silence behind all being is banished. The Enlightenment banished mystery and mysticism, relegating the latter to extraordinary states of consciousness on the periphery of things . . . [50]

When we purge our worlds of mystery we fill the empty space with ego. There can be no mysterious other force, only forces describable by the laws of physical science; mystery becomes no more than a lag in knowledge. There is nothing unknowable that can influence our lives. The belief that in principle all can be explored, understood and controlled is perhaps the quintessence of the Western apprehension of the world, it gives 'a specifically rational flavour' to the everyday experience of modern Western individuals, even those with little or no scientific training.[51] This influences our attitude to our worldly environment in the most profound way. It stands as an impenetrable barrier to the idea that the world has hidden meaning, that things bristle with intention, and that our lives can have a cosmic significance. Our isolated analytical selves have severed the links with the cosmos, have deprived the universe of meaning, and have in the process of self-assertion robbed us of our essential humanness. We are dead or, more optimistically, soundly asleep.

The need to know has developed historically from being an intellectual pursuit for a privileged few into an obsession of mass society. The idea that we obtain strength through knowledge has not always prevailed. In previous, more mystical ages people drew spiritual strength from the mystery of the universe. Jung noted this is his meetings with the Pueblo Indians of New Mexico, societies marked by their 'enviable serenity'. The Pueblo believe themselves to be the Sons of the Sun, the supporter of all life, and their rituals help the Sun traverse its daily path. Wrote Jung:

> if we . . . set aside our intimate knowledge of the world and exchange it for a horizon that seems immeasurable, and an ignorance of what lies beyond it, we will begin to achieve an inner comprehension of the Pueblo Indian's point of view.[52]

The idea of an infinite horizon strikes fear into our hearts, for it affirms our insignificance and our ignorance. It is dangerous for the rational mind to contemplate infinity. The need to know and control inheres in the psychology of our culture so deeply that we never question it. Thus the psychology of the Newtonian scientific revolution ushered in a new way of addressing our environment.

In economics the need to know provides the rationale for the profession, for greater knowledge means greater predictability and that in turn means greater control over the economy. This is quite contrary to an attitude which accepts and even welcomes the uncertainty of the future, an attitude that sits uncomfortably with *homo economicus*, a computer awaiting complete information. If one accepts the mystery then our behaviour as well as our attitudes change. We take actions that will promote our goals but we are willing to accept that the world is unpredictable. Rather than obsessively plan for contingencies, we acknowledge and welcome the spontaneity and joy of change that comes our way. Unpredicted events become opportunities.

In our endless attempts to secure our future, knowledge has acquired an enormous value. It seems that we can make ourselves happier through knowledge. At one level this is true, in the sense that greater knowledge of the possibilities can permit us greater freedom of choice and a greater knowledge of the outcomes of our decisions helps us make better decisions. But the pursuit of knowledge has conditioned our attitudes to knowledge and how we use it. Knowledge has become instrumental—it is useful solely because it enables us to do things, to act on the external world and control it. This is a very different concept of knowledge than that adopted in other cultures. That knowledge has value not because it is useful but because it influences our being, our sense of ourselves and how we fit into our world. It is knowledge that gives our lives solidity, sense and faith.

Erich Fromm, in his brilliant social analysis *To Have or to Be?*, discusses the way in which knowledge has become a commodity which is 'owned' by individuals. He distinguishes between 'having knowledge' and 'knowing'.

> *Having* knowledge is taking and keeping possession of available knowledge (information); *knowing* is functional and part of the process of productive thinking . . . . Knowing does not mean to be in possession of the truth; it means to penetrate the surface and to strive critically and actively in order to approach truth ever more closely.[53]

For great teachers such as the Buddha and Christ,

> the aim of knowing is not the certainty of 'absolute truth', something one can feel secure with, but *the self-affirming process of human reason.* Ignorance, for the one who knows, is as good as knowledge . . . . Optimum knowledge in the being mode is *to know more deeply.* In the having mode it is *to have more knowledge.*[54]

Fromm observes that our education systems are geared towards giving people more instrumental knowledge. The more 'having knowledge' people possess the higher is their social status and rewards. People are taught to feel valuable because they have more instrumental knowledge. Because knowledge confers social power it is treated as a precious commodity. Knowledge itself in the marketing society has become a tradeable commodity. The successful business person or bureaucrat learns early that control over information is control of power, and if one's aim is power and influence then information must be guarded—once it is known by one's opponents it loses its potency.

In recent years the economists have tackled the provision of education with the same calculus of monetary returns that they have attacked other areas. There have been proposals to provide school pupils or their parents with vouchers which they can then use to purchase the educational services they desire and can afford. As is the case in private universities, students buy the knowledge they want and are certified as possessing it. In this way students are thought to maximise the utility of the consumption of educational services subject to the constraint provided by the value of the vouchers.

Schools play a crucial role in reproducing the modern personality. While schools have a direct economic function in providing knowledge that allows students to acquire saleable skills in labour markets, they also train children to attach validity to rational thinking. While this is essential for good decision making, schools fail by teaching exclusively about the outside world, the world of reason. They shun the critical task of training children in self-knowledge, in understanding their inside worlds, and in developing other modes of thought—to accept intuition and to acknowledge their feelings as valid guides to action. In recent years the only way in which intuitive knowledge has crept into school syllabuses is through teaching children to trust their feelings when they are in danger of sexual abuse. Sensing this failing some parents insist on religious instruction, but to 'instruct' people in religion is a contradiction in terms.

Nowadays, information is packaged and sold as a commodity, especially through access to computer data banks. We are entering a new era, the era of information technology, which is sweeping all technologies before it. Information as a method of control is taking over service and manufacturing industries through computerisation, numerically controlled automation and robotics. But the vast expansion of information generating systems—collecting, processing and applying information—does not mean that we are getting any wiser. Indeed the technological control that the information revolution has permitted may have created more problems that we cannot deal with. It blinds us to the need to seek other forms of knowledge. While our societies are full of very knowledgeable people—people who have spent years, perhaps decades, learning—most are left ignorant of themselves and the world beyond that which can be apprehended by Cartesian rationality. They rarely learn to know themselves, nor to trust the knowledge they have within themselves, even though this knowledge is the distillation of centuries of human activity. The knowledge of the wise is self-knowledge, a knowledge that grows from accepting and understanding our inner experiences and thereby understanding the world which each of us, hologram-like, embodies. This is knowledge that can guide us in our lives rather than knowledge we have copied from others. In his poem *The Tables Turned*, Wordsworth contrasts the rational, transmissible knowledge of the 'sages' with the knowledge that may come to anyone from experiencing ourselves as universal beings, such as may be thrust upon us during a springtime walk through a forest.

> One impulse from a vernal wood
> May teach you more of man,
> Of moral evil and of good,
> Than all the sages can.

Our personal relationships to rational and symbolic knowledge differ. Rational knowledge can be transmitted from one person to another and can therefore be expropriated by one person or group of people for its own use. Wordsworth's knowledge stands in stark contrast to the empiricist attitude that knowledge is gained by mentally processing independent observations of the external world. In classical scientific method the correct procedure is for the experimenter to act on the external world and observe the results. Essentially the same method is used by economists. Knowledge is gathered on peoples' preferences by observing the impact of their expressed preferences on the world, that is, in marketplaces. Where these preferences are not expressed in market places, for example the 'preference' for a new area of wilderness, an experiment is conducted in which people are asked to express their preferences hypothetically or indirectly through other forms of market behaviour.

The idea of the independence of the observer has been questioned from a political point of view in the past, but the developments of quantum physics raise more fundamental questions. Capra observes that one of the most fundamental and difficult-to-accept implications of quantum physics is the need to abandon the idea of the independent observer. By observing the world we change it.

> My conscious decision about how to observe, say, an electron will determine the electron's properties to some extent. If I ask it a particle question, it will give me a particle answer; if I ask it a wave question, it will give me a wave answer. . . . In atomic physics the sharp Cartesian division between mind and matter, between the observer and the observed, can no longer be maintained.[55]

While the reasons for it may be quite different, the inseparability of the observed and the observer is even stronger in the social sciences. In economics, if we ask about preferences we will get an answer about preferences. But that does not mean that we have asked the right question or, more significantly, that the mode of questioning is adequate. The economists' questions reside in the domain of Fromm's 'having knowledge'. To the extent that we as humans live outside of the domain of rational calculation, the economists' analysis can only be a partial one. Experiential knowledge, on the other hand, arises only from direct, personal experience and as such it cannot be priced, privatised, expropriated, or marketed. It can in no way fit into the structure of modern economics.

Our society devalues experiential knowledge; we actively dismiss it, deny its validity, damn it as irrational. This is consistent with the fundamental desire to control, to exert power over the earth and other people. The realm of rational knowledge is the realm of control and power over the *external world*; the realm of experiential knowledge is the realm of acceptance and power over *oneself.*

The development of the ability to reason is a key phase in cognitive development and in the development of the ego. To a greater or lesser degree, individuals learn to identify their egos with rationality. For many, especially men, it becomes a critical part of their self-definition. We remember the stage of development at high school when we learned to argue rationally, when it became possible to win in a conflict with another by using reason. Many adolescents, especially boys, take to this form of thinking and discourse very strongly, becoming immersed in mathematical reasoning, playing chess and insisting that everything should be 'logical'. It has a great appeal and becomes a critical part of self-definition; it gives strength in a world that idolises reason. Perhaps for boys it is a part of the process of breaking away from their mothers. Undoubtedly, development of the powers of reason is a critical phase of child development. The tragedy of post-Enlightenment European culture has been that too many become stuck in that phase, failing to see the ability to reason as an important aspect of their lives and the world, but as only one aspect of human development. Problems arise when we become frozen in the stage of adolescent rationality, unable to move on to acceptance and understanding of deeper levels of knowledge and awareness. O'Connor writes of the 'twentieth-century obsession with rational thinking, empirical science and an almost childish belief in facts and a childish obsession with proof'.[56]

Reason is held up to be universal, external to all particular forms of humanity, and is therefore not specific to any person or culture. This perception runs counter to the anthropological evidence that culture conditions cognitive processes. Writing of his meeting with a chief of the Pueblo Indians in New Mexico, Jung reported that the Pueblos believed that white men were mad. When Jung asked why they believed whites are mad the chief replied: "They say they think with their heads. We think here", indicating his heart.[57] This understanding is paralleled in other mystical traditions (such as Hinduism and Kashmir Shaivism) in which the mind is experienced in the head only when it is cogitating, agitated, discriminating and judging. When the mind is stilled, through meditation for example, it resides in the heart centre. It is from there that great insight springs; that is where the intellect, the spirit and the emotions coincide. While our minds in our heads differentiate us as individuals, as small beings, our minds in our hearts link each of us to the collective consciousness, the ground of being.

One of the most pernicious side effects of our obsession with rationality is scepticism. It should be said at the outset that I am not suggesting that we should approach the world with an attitude of wide-eyed gullibility. There is, however, a middle position between scepticism and gullibility that allows us to explore the new and the mysterious, to accept that there are things we cannot understand. Scepticism serves to close off whole worlds of experience and levels of understanding. In particular, scepticism denies us the insight into the inner world of symbols and qualitative experience. Heraclitus in the 6th century BC wrote: 'What is divine escapes men's notice because of their incredulity.'[58] Our incredulity is a defence against fear. We fear confrontation with our own limits of understanding. In the inner world of symbols we meet things that go well beyond our powers of rational comprehension and our powers of control.

Scepticism is in many circles, notably in the scientific and economic professions, considered to be a highly desirable quality. We speak of so-and-so being 'such a cynic'. We regard this is a valuable quality because it means that they cannot be fooled. But the fear of appearing foolish reflects a profound lack of confidence in oneself, an enslavement to social norms, an unwillingness to accept the new and unfamiliar, an unwillingness to explore differing experiences and the ideas built on them. Cynicism is a psychology of rejection, a barrier we erect between ourselves and a world we see as untrustworthy. Rational constructions are the bricks and mortar of this barrier. At its core, however, it is a barrier against ourselves, against a world that reaches inside of us. Scepticism leaves a vacuum of trust within us.

The sceptic is in fact engaged in an endless war against himself. I say 'himself' because obsessive scepticism is largely a male preserve. The two worlds are within all of us, they are in our very natures as humans, and the inner world of symbols manifests itself relentlessly. Jung once wrote:

> It must be admitted that the archetypal contents of the collective unconscious can often assume grotesque and horrible forms in dreams and fantasies, so that even the most hard-boiled rationalist is not immune from shattering nightmares and haunting fears.[59]

Jung was once asked which people he found most difficult to heal. He answered unhesitatingly: 'habitual liars and intellectuals'.[60] Jung argued that the association of the two is not arbitrary. Intellectuals vest rational intellectual processes with omnipotence. When faced with the savage history of humankind and the day-to-day mysteries of human behaviour, the circumscribed nature of the arena of the intellect leaps out at us with irresistible force. The intellectual, then, is a kind of habitual liar because failing to admit the whole truth is a lie, a lie we tell ourselves. The whole truth encompasses not only the intellectual processes of humans but our numinous world, our world of unconscious motivations, the world of symbols.

BEYOND THE RATIONAL

I have traced out some of the elements of the historical emergence in the West of the dominance and eventually, in the twentieth century, the almost exclusive admissibility of the external world of material things. The triumph of the outer world was also the triumph of rationality. If the outside world is the only world that has validity, then the mode of discourse of the outside world, rationality, is the only valid mode of discourse. But if one can bring oneself to accept the validity of the internal world—and to do so is more an emotional struggle than an intellectual discovery—then one accepts that there is an internal mode of discourse. We shall call this internal mode of discourse *transrationality*.

In his study of the hierarchy of religious experience, the sociologist Ken Wilber notes the increasing reacceptance among developmental psychologists of the idea that there is a structural parallel between phylogenetic evolution—the history of the evolution of the human race—and ontogenetic evolution—the developmental path of the individual described in particular by the cognitive stages of Piaget. This idea is closely related to Jung's notion of the collective unconscious, the repository for the symbolic content of all human history which forms the hidden infrastructure of consciousness in each of us. Norman Brown reminds us of Freud's observation that in the few years of childhood 'we have to cover the enormous distance of development from primitive man of the Stone Age to civilized man of today'. 'Ontogeny recapitulates phylogeny', writes Brown.[61]

Wilber's hierarchy of religious experience suggests to him the phases of spiritual development and this in turn parallels the phases of cognitive development of each human being. Wilber's thesis is summarised in the following paragraphs, beginning with the earliest form of human consciousness.[62]

> Paleolithic humans had magic religion: totem ritual that expressed the confusion of human and animal ancestors, voodoo-like rituals, animistic beliefs, and so on.

This stage of human development corresponds to the pre-operational thinking stage of early childhood. Next,

> Neolithic and Bronze Age humans had classical mythic religion: gods and goddesses controlling their fate, with petitionary rituals and prayers offered by humans to their heavenly fathers and mothers.

This stage corresponds to the late childhood stage of pre-operational thinking and the beginning of concrete operational thinking.

> And then, finally, comes the revolution of rationality (starting with Greece c. sixth century B.C., reaching its stride with eighteenth-century Enlightenment thought but only today beginning to claim a clearly dominant structural role). [It is] the first structure that can not only think about the world but think about thinking . . . [and] the first structure capable of hypothetico-deductive or propositional reasoning ("if a, then b"), which allows it to apprehend higher or purely noetic relationships.

The age of reason corresponds to this last adolescent-to-adult stage of cognitive development, one of formal operational and deductive reasoning. This way of viewing the development of formal reasoning explains why psychologists, especially Jungians, refer sometimes to the 'childish' obsession with rationality that our society displays.

Although Wilber's characterisation of the processes of personal development and religious hierarchy remains hypothetical, the essential point of Wilber's argument is that the process does not necessarily stop at the age of reason. There are stages of thought-experience or levels of awareness that are beyond that of formal operational thinking, the stage which present Western civilization appears to have reached. Individuals possess the ability to develop beyond exclusively rational forms of apprehension; we each have the potential for transrational psychological structures. Wilber's idea of stages of consciousness that go beyond the rational is very familiar to the great Eastern psychological traditions, most notably those of Buddhism and Hinduism.

The discussion of symbols has already provided an idea of the content of transrational 'thought'. Because of our obsession with rationality, the transrational level in our society operates mostly at an unconscious level. The superiority of rational thought upon which Western opinion insists has meant that other forms of apprehension of the world are generally suppressed, driven into our unconscious minds or entertained consciously only in private. Transrational thought includes the sudden intuitions that inspire both scientific discovery and deep personal understanding. It is the radical insight into the nature of things; the identification that bestows participatory knowledge, the knowledge that dissolves the separation of the knower and the known. It is our state of consciousness when we are seized by compassion. When we feel, and at some level understand, an affinity with our natural environment, or when we are profoundly moved by a piece of music or art, or have a sense of unity with something greater than ourselves yet part of ourselves, then we experience a transrational apprehension of the world. This is not mere emotionalism, although strong emotions may accompany these cognitions, but grows out of an awareness of ourselves-beyond-ourselves.

The problem with modern economics is not so much that it operates purely at the level of the rational (though of course many would argue that it is not rational enough); the problem with modern economics is that it reinforces society's insistence on the sole validity of rationality to the exclusion of all else. The irony is that no matter how hard economic rationality may try it cannot suppress the symbolic world because the world is in its essence symbolic. We are each prerational, rational and transrational. That is why no matter how much we may want to run our lives according to the rules of rationality alone, and no matter how sceptical we are about manifestations of the numinous world, each of us is an expression of the cosmic whole. That is why everything is sacred. Insistence on exclusive rationality makes us prone to forget the fact. The urges that lay beneath the rituals of sacrifice and of the hunt that characterised the economic activities of traditional societies also underlie the money exchange and consumer strivings of today. The profane, then, is only another manifestation of the sacred. That is why the modern economy, for all of its profanity, is also sacred. Our task is to go beyond the profane exterior to a conscious acceptance of the sacredness of daily life. For to go beyond the economist within is to begin to go beyond the ego-identification that binds us to the world of separation and struggle.

1 Morris Berman, *The Reenchantment of the World* (Cornell University Press, Ithaca, 1981), p. 16

2 Quoted by Joseph Campbell, *The Power of Myth* (Doubleday, New York, 1988) p. 34. Theodore Roszak notes that the quote may be more apocryphal than historically accurate (*The Voice of the Earth*, Simon and Schuster, New York, 1992).

3 Johann Goethe, *Faust* (Penguin, London, 1949) Part 1, p. 145

4 Ken Wilber, *Up From Eden: A Transpersonal View of Human Evolution* (New Science Library, Shambhala, Boston, 1986) p. 41. Some of Wilber's arguments are developed from Ernest Becker's startling work *Escape From Evil* (The Free Press, New York, 1975). Becker writes:

'As I see it, the history of mankind divides into two great periods: the first one existed from time immemorial until roughly the Renaissance or Enlightenment, and it was characterized by the ritualistic view of nature. The second period began with the efflorescence of the modern machine age and the domination of the scientific method and world view. In both periods men wanted to control life and death, but in the first period they had to rely on a nonmachine technology to do it . . . ' (p. 8).

5 Wilber, *op. cit.*, p. 42

6 Mircea Eliade, *The Forge and the Crucible: The Origins and Structures of Alchemy* (Harper & Row, New York, 1971)

7 Karl Marx and Friedrich Engels, *The Communist Manifesto* in Robert Tucker (ed.), *The Marx-Engels Reader,* (W.W. Norton & Company, New York, 1972) p. 337

8 Max Weber makes this point in *Economy and Society* (Bedminster Press, New York, 1968) p. 376

9 Eliade, *op. cit.*

10 'There are only two stations at which men and women are perfectly content. One is slumbering in the subconscious, the other is awakened as the superconscious. Everything in between is various degrees of pandemonium. But hundreds of thousands of years ago, mankind took courage and stepped out of the slumber of Eden, renounced its sleep in the subconscious, abandoned its life with the lilies of the field, and began the slow climb back to the superconscious All. It abandoned the life of the sleeping serpent uroboros, abandoned the pre-personal stage shared with the rest of nature, and became, of all the animals, the Prodigal Son lost in the wilderness.' (Ken Wilber, *Up From Eden, op. cit.*, p. 111) The idea that humans once lived in a state of serenity and will do so again is common to mythologies around the globe.

11 Jean Liedloff, *The Continuum Concept* (Gerald Duckworth & Co., London, 1975)

12 Wilber, *op cit.*, p. 41, my emphasis

13 Berman, *op. cit.*, p. 166

14 Joseph Campbell quoted by Wilber, *op. cit.*, pp. 77–78

15 Richard Bucke, *Cosmic Consciousness* (Dutton & Co., New York, 1969)

16 Berman, *op. cit.*, pp. 112–113

17 Berman, *op. cit.*, p. 123

18 Berman, *op. cit.*, p. 126

19 See Max Weber, *op. cit.*

20 On Weber's analysis see Rogers Brubaker, *The Limits to Rationality* (George Allen and Unwin, London, 1984), especially pp. 10–16. This passage is from p. 10.

21 Weber, *op. cit.*, p. 86

22 Fritjof Capra, *The Tao of Physics* (Shambhala, Berkeley, 1975) p. 44

23 Capra's discussion of this is particularly lucid; see especially Fritjof Capra, *The Turning Point* (Fontana, London, 1983) pp. 48–49 and 50.

24 Capra, *The Tao of Physics, op. cit.*, p. 44

25 Capra, *The Tao of Physics, op. cit.*, p. 45

26 Capra, *The Tao of Physics, op. cit.*, p. 28

27 Weber, *op. cit.*, pp. 91–92

28 Weber, *op. cit.*, p. 92. Brubaker provides a very interesting commentary on Weber, including the following:

'These specific characteristics of modern capitalism converge on the idea of calculability—not, however, the calculability inherent in the use of money, but a much more thoroughgoing calculability based on the technique of capital accounting, on rigorous factory discipline and the precise control by owners of all human and non-human means of production, on a predictable legal and administrative system, and on the "extension of productivity of labor . . . through the subordination of the process of production to scientific points of view".' (Brubaker, *op. cit.*, p. 12)

29 See, for example, Stephen Hawking, *A Brief History of Time* (Bantam Books, Toronto, 1988).

30 Capra, *The Tao of Physics, op. cit.*, p. 65

31 See Hawking, *op. cit.* and Capra, *The Tao of Physics, op. cit.*

32 Carl Jung, *Psychology and Alchemy*, Collected Works, Volume 12 (Routledge & Kegan Paul, London, 1953)

33 Jung, *ibid.*, p. 34. Also, 'The free-ranging psyche of the adept used chemical substances and processes as a painter uses colours to shape out the images of his fancy.' Carl Jung, *Mysterium*

Coniunctionis, Collected Works, Volume 14, Second edition (Routledge & Kegan Paul, London, 1970), p. 483

34 Eliade, *op. cit.*, p. 119. Jung wrote: 'In the face of all this one is driven to the conjecture that medieval alchemy, which evolved out of the Arabic tradition sometime in the thirteenth century . . . was in the last resort a continuation of the doctrine of the Holy Ghost, which never came to very much in the Church.' (Jung, *Mysterium Coniunctionis, op. cit.*, p. 318)

35 Eliade, *op. cit.*, p. 162

36 Berman, *op. cit.*, p. 73

37 Berman, *op. cit.*, p. 99

38 Berman, *op. cit.*, pp. 95 & 121

39 Although he was attacked by the Astronomer Royal for his occult beliefs.

40 R.S. Westfal reported in Berman, *op. cit.*, p. 125

41 Jung, *Mysterium, op. cit.*, p. 468

42 Goethe, *Faust, op. cit.*, p. 45

43 Eliade, *op. cit.*, pp. 143–44

44 'The production of caelum is a symbolic rite performed in the laboratory. Its purpose was to create, in the form of a substance, that "truth", the celestial balsam or life principle, which is identical with the God-image. Psychologically, it was a representation of the individuation process by means of chemical substances and procedures, or what we today call active imagination.' (Jung, *Mysterium, op. cit.*, p. 494)

45 Arthur Koestler, *The Sleepwalkers*, (Penguin, Harmondsworth, 1964) p. 37

46 Koestler, *ibid.*, pp. 520–21

47 Koestler, *ibid.*, p. 523

48 Berman, *op. cit.*, p. 139

49 Berman, *op. cit.*, p. 157

50 Matthew Fox, *The Coming of the Cosmic Christ* (Collins Dove, Melbourne, 1988) p. 77

51 Brubaker, *op. cit.*, p. 31

52 Carl Jung, *Memories, Dreams, Reflections* (Fontana, London, 1983) p. 281

53 Erich Fromm, *To Have or to Be?* (Abacus, London, 1979) pp. 47-48

54 Fromm, *ibid.*, p. 48

55 Capra, *The Turning Point, op. cit.*, p. 77

56 Peter O'Connor, *Understanding Jung, Understanding Yourself* (Methuen Haynes, 1985) pp. 142–43

57 Jung, *Memories, op. cit.,* p. 276

58 Quoted by Berman, *op. cit.,* p. 95

59 Jung, *Psychology and Alchemy, op. cit.,* p. 32

60 Laurens van der Post, *Jung and the Story of Our Time* (Vintage Books, New York, 1977) p. 133

61 Norman O. Brown, *Life Against Death* (Wesleyan University Press, Middletown, Connecticut, 1959) p. 13. Brown continues with a remarkable statement: 'the theory of neurosis must embrace a theory of history; and conversely a theory of history must embrace a theory of neurosis'. This is the essential idea underlying the present work, *viz.* a theory of the emergence of an industrial society with a corresponding theory of the specific neurosis described by the idea of 'rational economic man' or *homo economicus.*

62 Ken Wilber, *A Sociable God: Towards A New Understanding of Religion* (New Science Library, Shambhala, Boulder, 1984), especially Chapter 2.

7 ENVIRONMENTALISM AND MYSTICISM

The modern environment movement represents an opportunity for humankind, and especially Western civilisation, to recapture a mystical relationship with the natural world. Here I want to argue that the success of environmentalism in its quest is essential not only to our material well being but, more importantly, to our psychological health. To reach this conclusion there are four points I would like to make.

First, I argue that mystical experience is an inescapable part of being human. Secondly, experience of the mystery and wildness of the natural world has historically been essential to experiencing life fully. This is because the external wilderness corresponds to and sustains the wilderness within.

Thirdly, the filling up of the Earth by human activity has brought about the loss of Nature's sacredness. The loss of Nature has made us painfully alienated from the wilderness within. Modern economics relentlessly reinforces this alienation from self. A most fundamental part of ourselves—a part that is essential to experiencing ourselves as whole beings—has become inaccessible.

Lastly, it is argued that the environment movement is an attempt not only to prevent the degradation and destruction of the physical world but, at a deeper level, an attempt to reverse the historical alienation from ourselves, to reestablish a mystical relationship with the world. It is not so much a question of saving Nature so that we can have mystical experiences. Rather, due to our essentially mystical nature we sense that the destruction of the natural world is the destruction of ourselves.

I want to go beyond the logical, scientific discourse of the environmental debate, beyond the potential catastrophes of the physical world, and explore the catastrophe of the inner world. I want to explore how ecology, as a reassertion of our unity with the natural world, can serve as a way out of the prison of scientific reason and into a richer world of mysterious forces and symbols, the numinous world that has always given meaning to human life. By no means do I maintain that we should abandon science and reason, only that we diminish ourselves and our potentialities by clinging onto rationality to the exclusion of other forms of awareness.

WHAT IS MYSTICISM?

Mysticism has a bad name nowadays. It appears to run directly contrary to the essential thrust of Western thought since the European Enlightenment which has been to establish rationality and science as the sole legitimate means of understanding and thus appropriating the world. The word 'mysticism' is now used as an insult. It is employed to refer to unscientific, illogical thinking, to describe people who believe in things that manifestly do not exist. If I am to defend mysticism, then, I should first make clear what I mean by it.

Quotation of dictionary definitions is usually boring, but in this case the Oxford English Dictionary gives such a precise yet provocative definition that I must refer to it. The OED defines a mystic as follows:

> *Mystic:* One who seeks by contemplation and self-surrender to obtain union with or absorption into the Deity, or who believes in spiritual apprehension of truths beyond understanding.

What an extraordinary statement this is; what strange concepts—'self-surrender', 'union with the Deity', 'spiritual apprehension', 'truths beyond understanding'. They describe a world that is the complete opposite of the conventional world in which we are schooled, the world of science and reason in which truths and understanding are established by independent subjects making observations about an objective external world. In a world that makes an emphatic distinction between ourselves as beings and the world in which we live, what can it mean to surrender the self to the Deity? These phrases seem to imply above all the dissolution of the boundaries between ourselves and the world around us, the abolition of the distinction between ourselves as individuals and the cosmos in which we exist. They therefore challenge the very notions of the objectivity, the rationality and the discreteness of the individual that are the foundations of the Western scientific vision, of Western economics and of Western thought itself.

It is odd that mysticism has such a bad name, for these ideas and practices have an ancient and respectable lineage. All of the great religious teachers—Buddha, Mohammed, Lao Tse, Jesus Christ—were avowed mystics. They practised meditation, prayer and devotion as a means of achieving union with God or merger with the Absolute and they spoke in parables or abstractions that touched truths beyond rational proof. The modern-day rejection of mysticism is a rejection of what these great mystics preached; in place of spiritual truths and pursuit of union with the Deity we have substituted science, materialism and economics.

On what grounds do I claim that we are mystical beings? Firstly, we are mystical beings because the great teachers say we are, and they are great teachers because at some level we, individually and collectively, recognise the truth of what they say. In addition, all of us at certain times in our lives experience the world mystically. Mostly we choose to ignore these radical insights because they appear to be so difficult to reconcile, intellectually and emotionally, with a strict scientific view of the world and because we are not taught how to understand them otherwise. Birth and death are intensely mystical experiences, although we generally either cannot remember them or are not around to proclaim them. But sometimes, as in rebirthing experiences and near-death experiences, we survive to reflect on them and talk about them.

The everyday accessibility of mystical experience can be illustrated by the story of a man who worked in a government research bureau. Although a solid civil servant, Peter had a beard and wore hiking boots to work. His passion was bushwalking. Once in Tasmania, he and his two friends were three days out from civilisation, walking with the meditative rhythm of the seasoned bushwalker. As he walked along a cliff top, Peter suddenly broke through the barrier. The whole world somehow shifted and he walked in it rather than on it. His mind was no longer an organ of cognition but the seat of a consciousness that spread seamlessly into the world around him. His living consciousness, his essence as a being, had been absorbed into the cosmos; the boundaries had simply dissolved. Peter was transported from the mundane world as he walked and was given an unforgettable flash of insight into the true nature of things. But too soon the reflective, frightened analytical mind restarted and his state of cosmic absorption evaporated instantly. In order to move in and out of this state at will, yogis practice for many years to attain an advanced level of enlightenment. Ordinary householders like us are afraid when we break through the barrier and, just by thinking about it, we separate ourselves from the state of blissful unity.

THE SACREDNESS OF NATURE

The historian of religion Mircea Eliade, in his book *The Sacred and the Profane*, provides intriguing insights into the sacredness of nature in traditional religious life.

> For religious man, nature is never only "natural"; it is always fraught with a religious value. . . . . All this is not arrived at by a logical, rational operation. [It] is revealed to the whole man, to his intelligence and his soul. . . . . Experience of a radically desacralized nature is a recent discovery; moreover, it is an experience accessible only to a minority in modern societies, especially to scientists. For others, nature still exhibits a charm, a mystery, a majesty in which it is possible to decipher traces of ancient religious values. No modern man, however irreligious, is entirely insensible to the charms of nature.[1]

These words could describe the worldview of Native Americans—such as has been articulated so forcefully and beautifully by Chief Seattle—or the cosmology of Australian Aborigines. And although we have all but forgotten it, it is the heritage of Europeans, an awareness driven from our conscious understanding only in the last two or three hundred years.

As Carl Jung, Mircea Eliade, Joseph Campbell and several others have shown in their studies of depth psychology, the history of religion and the role of myths, the deepest structures of our psyches are the oldest. It took two million years for us to form as humans, and at the deepest levels of our beings we today are the same as we were ten thousand years ago.

Stimulated by environmentalism, there has been a surge of interest in the US in the religious ways of life of Native Americans. We recounted in Chapter 4 the myth of the Blackfoot, a plains tribe, that tells how the original Blackfoot entered into a pact with the buffalo, their source of livelihood.[2] The buffalo graciously agreed to sacrifice themselves to feed the Blackfoot as long as the Blackfoot performed the sacred song and dance of the buffalo after each kill. The ritual served to bring the dead buffalo back to life and thereby to maintain the cosmic balance between humans and their environment, and to remind the hunters of the sacred duty of humility before Nature.

Ritual and religion had very practical benefits in maintaining ecological harmony. The buffalo myth of the Blackfoot affirmed the unity of humans and their natural environment and warned against the separation and arrogance that leads people to believe that they can just take from the land without the corresponding responsibility to nurture it. This is why it is an error of modern civilisation to regard myths as untrue; myths always convey a powerful psychological truth.

Campbell's observations on the impact of the slaughter of the buffalo by white hunters, an image so powerfully captured in the film *Dances With Wolves*, may serve as a grim warning. For the North American plains tribes, the wiping out of the buffalo meant more than the loss of their principal source of food. The activity that was the core of the myths that established their relationship with the world, that was the religious symbol that gave meaning to life, was gone. The peyote cult that swept up from Mexico could no more substitute for the spiritual bonding of the 'buffalo religion' than LSD in the 1960s could fill the spiritual emptiness left by official Christianity.

Even for Westerners, after 300 years of scientific rationalism and the industrial ego, the sacredness of special places sometimes seeps into our consciousnesses. The mining dispute at Coronation Hill in Northern Australia (see Chapter 4) was influenced by more than Aboriginal claims that the hill is a sacred site. The special feel of the 'Sickness Country' that surrounds the hill affects white people too. Europeans who visit the area find themselves unsettled by a sense of presence: the rocks emanate a subtle power; the trees and animals and birds seem to know; to visit that place is spontaneously to meditate. Even the executives of the mining companies, when at the site, are apologetic when explaining the benefits of mining. The Aboriginal notion of 'country' remains vestigially in the bones of Europeans. Once all of the land—its trees, rivers and wildlife—had a sacred quality. Now we have desacralized the land by building cities over it. We choose to live in these cities and that allows us to suppress the ancient sense of the sacredness of the land.

THE WORLD FILLED UP

Herman Daly has recently pointed out that humans currently appropriate 40 per cent of the net product of the Earth's land-based photosynthesis (the process that combines sunlight with organic materials to produce plant growth). Seventy years ago we used up only 10 per cent and, if current rates of conversion of land continue, in 35 years we will consume 80 per cent. Daly says that this represents a transition from a world that was relatively empty of human activity to one that is full, indeed overfull.[3]

Today, almost the entire area of the Earth's crust is managed by humans; very few areas remain that are wild and impenetrable. Wilderness must now be 'managed' in an attempt to prevent these last areas from being overrun by human intervention. But, of course, management itself is a method of human intervention. Expeditions now venture to Mount Everest to clean up the empty cans left by climbers. The Antarctic is blighted by dumps filled with domestic waste and leaking oil drums. Park rangers in the wilderness of South West Tasmania complain of the litter left by East European tourists. In the remote geocentre of the island of Borneo, dirt-poor workers at a logging camp watch 'MacGyver' on satellite television.

There is now enormous concern about the implications of this bloated growth; and it is a bandwagon that everyone should jump onto. Western environmentalism has produced many excellent utilitarian reasons for repairing the damage and taking care of the natural environment more responsibly. Environmentalists have forced us to confront the question of whether our standards of living can be maintained in a world of finite resources, and to see the damage we are doing to our well-being by pollution of the elements.

But something has been missed in the public debate, something that goes very deep, to our core as humans—and that is the impact on our psyches of the filling up of the Earth's surface.

When the world was relatively empty, that is for the first two million years of human history—until one or two hundred years ago—humans lived in communities that were islands of domestication in vast seas of wilderness. The world beyond the bounds of village or town was full of unknown terrors, but it was also the domain of the gods. This structure of the world laid down the foundations of the psyche. The wild woods, the mysterious mountains, the endless oceans—in short, the world beyond the known—gave humans a place where the world beyond the barrier could reside. It provided something onto which to project our shadow selves, the dark unknown within, the secrets of Pandora's box. It gave us a respect for mystery and a psychological balance that mirrored the intercourse of the conscious and the unconscious.

The impact of the great explorers who mapped out new trading routes was as much psychological as economic, for they began to link all parts of the world and to destroy forever the idea that the world 'outside' was unknown. The maps could no longer be drawn with dragons at the edges of the seas. As the rest of the world became 'known' it lost its mythic appeal and its terror; the world of the gods shrank. The work of the explorers was not just to turn the Earth into a known entity, but to lay the foundations of a global system that now links the fate of Colombian coffee farmers to the vagaries of European bourses and that subjects the psyches of Borneo's Dayak Indians to the neuroses of US television producers.

Now almost the entire surface of the Earth has been 'tamed'; all parts of the Earth will soon be managed by humans. The era of human domination is an extremely recent one, stretching back only a few decades, the last of thousands of decades of human history. The loss of the wilderness without threatens to rob us of the wilderness within, the inborn source of awareness of the cosmos that can keep us balanced and sane. Just as humanity evolved from creatures that crawled from the sea, in each of us modern consciousness has its ground in the sea of the unconscious. Without the material counterpart of the primal unconscious how are we to sustain ourselves psychologically? Under the dual onslaught of economic exploitation and scientific explanation, the world has lost its magic. We have nowhere to send Jason on his odyssey, except perhaps to outer space. If the world is wholly known or knowable then we can no longer participate in its mystery and indeed its consciousness; we can only observe it and analyse it with our conscious minds. What an inadequate substitute that is.

We hail the great European explorers—Columbus, Captain Cook, Edmund Hilary, Neil Armstrong—but at the same time we cling to the bits of the world that have escaped our physical control or domination by knowledge. We keep alive the stories of the Loch Ness monster and the yetis of the world. We are captivated by the lure of the dolphin who has calmly put itself beyond our reach, by the archetype of the untamable stallion, and by the wild woods of Tolkein. So there is a great conflict inside of us; for on the one hand we are driven to explore the world, to know it, to turn it to our own selfish ends, on the other we honour and admire it for refusing to succumb. We know that as we conquer Nature we are both increased and diminished. Each wilderness tamed, each species extinguished, each forest cut down means a loss without and a grief within.

ECONOMICS AS DENIAL

The new psychic barrenness that grew out of the European Enlightenment and the scientific revolution was expressed most perfectly by neoclassical economics in the figure of *homo economicus* or rational economic man. That is why, for all of its rationality and self-proclaimed objectivity, economics has a great deal to tell us about religion. Just as the man who hates his mother and the man who obsessively loves his mother are both driven by their mothers, economics is driven by its relationship to religion.

Rational economic man is the epitome of the separated individual who acts objectively on the world. According to this worldview, we as humans are defined quintessentially as isolated egos existing inside our bodies, to borrow Fritjof Capra's phrase. We are thus set up in opposition to the world around us. What can *homo economicus* do but attempt to control the world? This is so deep within our psyches that we rarely glimpse it. The tourists who flock to Uluru—previously known as Ayers Rock, that great primordial monolith in the centre of continental Australia—naturally want to climb to the top, a daily manifestation of the conquering spirit. The traditional Aboriginal owners have no urge to climb. The urge to climb Uluru is the same restless urge that now sees humankind controlling almost all of the Earth's surface and turning 40 per cent of plant growth to human use.

To control the world we transform its bounty into items of consumption. This we are told is the way to happiness; but it is predicated on the very separation from the world and is thus the source of our emptiness. Even Herman Daly has repeated the conventional view that if resources were infinite then economic growth would unreservedly be a good thing. Beyond meeting our basic needs, it is manifestly untrue that those who have been the beneficiaries of economic growth are better off because of it. Growth has become an obsession in the West where material enrichment is a vain attempt to fill the spiritual void.

We are what we meditate on. As we meditate on material enrichment we deny the spiritual self that defines us as human. The preoccupation of economics with maximising utility from consumption is simultaneously a denial of our true natures. The counterpart of the obsession with economic growth is separation from the natural world, one that causes us to treat it as a catalogue of resources that exist to be exploited. Whether resources are finite or not is irrelevant from this point of view. An infinity of resources is only more likely to extend the period in which we delude ourselves with the belief that the path to contentment lies in the accumulation of goods. This is the difference between environmental economics and the embryonic ecological economics. Environmental economics is a mere extension, without apology, of the old economics to incorporate some new elements into the 'utility functions' of the individual consumer. There is nothing new. The nascent approach of ecological economics abandons the imperialism of the old economics and begins from our unity with the natural world rather than our separation from it. Ecological economics may be on the verge of taking the most critical step—seeing humanity not merely as part of a cybernetic interdependent system but existing in mystical union with the natural world.

Initially I was appalled to read that the 1992 Nobel Prize for economics had been awarded to Gary Becker. I was astonished that a group of eminent Swedes could give such an accolade to an economist who epitomizes, more than any other, the imperialistic arrogance of the discipline of economics. Here was the economist who had explained crime, drug addiction and marriage as the products of rational utility maximising behaviour. Here was the economist who defined love as a 'non-marketable household commodity' and marriage as an arrangement to secure the mutual benefit of exchange between two agents of different endowments. Nothing could be more damaging to the environment than to apply the solutions of conventional economics, as elaborated with such extraordinary tenacity by Becker, to the issue of 'resource scarcity'. But perhaps it is better to see the Nobel award as the last hurrah of a dying creed. Modern economics is a dazzling intellectual edifice, but it is precisely the madness of the Becker project—to make the whole world in the image of rational economic man—that is bringing it crashing to the ground.

The imposition of economic rationality on all areas of human life is an increasingly desperate attempt to deny the unconscious, to dispel the uncomfortable mystery of the unknown and replace it by the light of conscious reason. But of course it can never succeed, because to have a conscious world balanced by the instinctual and numinous world of the unconscious (both its divine and shadow sides) is simply to be human. Carl Jung was most acutely aware of this. We referred previously to Jung's observation that the sometimes 'grotesque and horrible' contents of the unconscious burst into the lives of even the most hard-boiled rationalist in the forms of 'shattering nightmares and haunting fears'.[4] The extension of the domain of economic rationality to the messy worlds of family behaviour and social delinquency can only be seen as a pathetic attempt by some of the most hard-boiled rationalists to exorcise their own ghosts.

MODERN ENVIRONMENTALISM AS MYSTICISM

The modern environment movement has two objectives—to prevent the irretrievable transformation of the natural world and to reestablish, in the light of modern consciousness, our primordial unity with Nature. An environmentalist is 'one who seeks to obtain union with the Deity' where the deity is Gaia, the modern symbol that unites the inner with the outer, that transcends the boundaries.

While many modern-day environmentalists have mystical motivations, it is often difficult for them to admit it because the dominant modes of thought are so contemptuous of all things mystical, of anything outside of the bounds of the rational as conventionally defined. Although most environmentalists may not think of themselves as mystics their language and motivations often express their mystical connectedness. Deep ecology is most explicit about this with its insistence that Nature has intrinsic values beyond all human relationship. Or rather, so as not to abolish humans altogether, it is better to say that the intrinsic values of Nature (as opposed to the utilitarian values of economics and business) arise out of the dissolution of the subject-object relationship and its replacement by a consciousness of merger. What can this mean except that there is a world beyond the mundane material world of scientific analysis and economic calculation?

There is a modern story of a man who found himself in Nature, a story that stands, I believe, as a symbol of the deeper purpose of environmentalism, the quest to rediscover psychic wholeness in a society ravaged by spiritual emptiness. It was a story about Aldo Leopold, one of the founding thinkers of the philosophy of modern environmentalism in the USA. In order to escape from war, Leopold trekked into the Canadian wilderness. After weeks of lonely hiking into the remotest parts of Canada he came upon a grassy meadow. In the meadow he found a cluster of beautiful little yellow flowers. Overwhelmed by the realisation that such exquisite beauty could exist for its own sake, oblivious of human consciousness, he collapsed through the barrier of separation and drank the divine essence of the universe. He cried the humble tears of mystical knowledge, the tears of those whose painful journey ends in discovery of the Holy Grail.

While the scientific case for conservation must continue to be argued, the fundamental strength of environmentalism is drawn from its ethical commitment and spiritual knowledge. In different ways, many people in the modern environment movement have learnt the knowledge that Leopold found in the

Canadian wilderness. I hope that we can have the courage to proclaim that knowledge openly without fear of ridicule, so that we can declare ourselves to be both scientists and mystics, and from that acknowledgement speak to the whole of humanity.

1 Mircea Eliade, *The Sacred and the Profane* (Harcourt, Brace, Javanovich, New York 1959), pp. 116, 119, 151

2 Joseph Campbell, *Myths to Live By* (Bantam Books, New York 1973) pp. 37–40

3 Herman Daly, 'From empty-world to full-world economics' in Robert Goodland *et al.* (eds), *Environmentally Sustainable Economic Development: Building on Brundtland* (Unesco, Paris, 1991) p. 30

4 Carl Jung, *Psychology and Alchemy* (Princeton University Press, Princeton 1968) p. 32

8 ECONOMICS, ECOLOGY AND GOD

Deep within each of us lies a divine Self. The purpose of life is to find this Self and to live our lives from it. But the world of modern economics acts unceasingly to obscure our divine Selves from our conscious awareness. The world of modern economics—the ideas and the institutions and the behaviours it prescribes—entangles us in the world of a thousand things and encourages our baser desires; devotion to it prevents us from recognizing and pursuing the purpose of life on Earth.

Although dressed in modern guise, this is the eternal wisdom of the sages, sages from all spiritual traditions through the centuries. If the reader is offended by these propositions, I ask only that you listen intuitively to the argument of this tract, as much with the heart as with the mind. It is often the case that excessive analysis with the rational mind, the hallmark of the economist's trade, is the most effective means of resisting a truth known by the heart.

The great struggle of modern humankind—three centuries after the onset of the scientific-industrial revolution—is to transcend our crippling obsession with rationality and to rediscover the harmonious power of our intuitive knowledge, the only means by which we can know god.

THE MODERN INDIVIDUAL

The critique of the world of neoclassical economics, the overwhelmingly dominant school of economics, begins and ends with the perception of what we are as beings. In essence, the modern economist's definition of the self and the true Self—the divine Self—are utterly incompatible, and so long as we identify with the economist's individual we are doomed to live out lives of restlessness and discontent.

The Western notion of the individual, as a distinct being with certain innate motivations, is a very modern invention. Prior to the European Enlightenment and the scientific-industrial revolution, the prevailing concept of the person was an organic one. While the material conditions of life were for most people far less lavish than they are today, each person felt more a sense of unity of spirit with the natural world and the cosmos. This unity expressed both the sense that we are part of the universe, and the sense that the universe is part of us.

In Europe, as elsewhere, people perceived the world around them as enchanted. The animals, the sky, the hills and the sun vibrated with the shared energy of existence, and merger with this force provided a true home for the human spirit. In the words of Morris Berman,

> The cosmos . . . was a place of belonging. A member of this cosmos was not an alienated observer of it but a direct participant in its drama. His personal destiny was bound up with its destiny, and this relationship gave meaning to his life.[1]

The psychological implications of this view of the world could not be more profound.

> This type of consciousness . . . involves merger, or identification, with one's surroundings, and bespeaks a psychic wholeness that has long since passed from the scene.[2]

The advent of industrial society brought about a transformation at the deepest levels of human awareness. There emerged a sense of the self as an *isolated ego* existing inside our bodies, a sense of self in which 'I in here' act on 'the world out there'. With this grew the entirely new idea, so fundamental to our behaviour, that our activities directed at the inert external world determine our fate. In short, there developed the modern idea of the individual.

Industrial technology was a critical contribution to this psychological transition. Technological advance gradually led us to believe that we could control and dominate the natural world. Our fate became our own responsibility. Tragically, we could not cultivate the psychological strength to shoulder this appalling burden and we have been bequeathed a life in which we, like Sisyphus, must labour at our task in a world that relentlessly undoes our efforts.

The onslaught of rational thinking was employed to destroy 'primitive' beliefs that had served previously to give meaning to human lives. If magic gave meaning, the abolition of magic meant the loss of meaning. Peace could be had only by providing a new relationship with the cosmos that served the functions of the old. The new relationship was a scientific-industrial programme designed to seize control of the world and turn it to our own ends. The natural world, the cosmos itself, was taken apart and reconstructed on the belief that everything is explainable, so that there could be nothing of substance left to the gods. Eternal mysteries became temporarily unsolved problems; and the humility that rewards us with cosmic harmony was gone.

But a world without the gods could only work if it truly were knowable and could be brought to heel by the combined might of human will and human intellect. This was the dangerous pass to which the loss of innocence had led. The new science provided not only the opportunity to comprehend the laws of the physical world but a new personality to go with it, the industrial ego.

The new science provided both the key to the transformation of the physical world and the essential rationale for the reconceptualization of Nature—its division into a catalogue of resources whose values arise not from direct appreciation of Nature but from the possibility of exploiting it. Science itself, by means of the analytical method, prefigured the physical death of the world. If humans truly are at one with the natural world then a dead world means a dead inner self. In the words of a witness to the transition, the mystic poet Wordsworth:

> Our meddling intellect
> Misshapes the beauteous forms of things:-
> We murder to dissect.

The change in the perception of the world, this scientific consciousness, opened the way for an epoch-making transformation of the human psyche. If one perceives the world with a *participating* consciousness—immersed in a world that is magical and alive and full of intentions—then a certain humility is inescapable. The arrogant, rational ego of the modern world could only stand tall once the world was dead and appeared to offer no resistance to manipulation.

The scientific-industrial revolution and the rise of rationalism, then, robbed the world of its magic; but it was only we who were deprived. Our own last links with the natural world were severed and we were left floating in the cosmos, searching for an anchor, yearning for a meaning, terrorized by our emptiness, seeking a return to the universal fold.

THE NEW ECONOMICS

The new science of economics accurately mirrored the emergence of the objective individual newly divorced from the living, vibrating, intentioned world. It took as its task the analysis, strictly by mode of rational discourse, of a dead world peopled by economic agents.

Modern economics set out from the idea that the economic agent is above all else an individual. An economy is defined as an aggregation of individuals who interact with each other through mathematically specified forms of economic behaviour. Each individual is distinguished by a set of tastes or desires that are expressed in the marketplace through a 'utility function'. The utility function is a representation of the process whereby a bundle of commodities purchased in the marketplace by a consumer is translated into a measure of 'welfare' or happiness. The aim in life of economic agents is to maximize their welfare by spreading their limited income across the range of goods available at given prices. This is the sum and substance of Chapter One of all neoclassical economics textbooks. In the archetypal economic situation the consumer, a self-contained individual defined by a set of preferences and a set of endowments, confronts an array of goods with the aim of maximizing his or her welfare. From this starting point, the modern economist interprets the world as a giant calculating machine and within this machine economic agents provide the computing power that ensures that an optimal solution always emerges.

The economists' idea of the individual inheres deeply in our own intellectual and emotional perceptions of ourselves. Indeed, so deeply does it inhere that it seems indisputable that it should be the starting point for understanding the mundane world. The economists' individual, known as *homo economicus*, is above all an isolated ego existing inside a body. Is this not what we really are? Who can deny that I experience myself as an isolated ego inside my body? But this unchallengeable truth is in reality a very modern and highly culturally specific perception of the self, as Joseph Campbell, in his studies of the myths of the world, has shown beyond any doubt.[3] Of course, when pressed, modern economics recognizes that individuals are in some respects social products: their tastes are formed, in large measure, by social pressures; preferences may include preferences for social goods; and markets are collective institutions. But for economics all of this is mere prehistory. At any point in time, the individual stands alone, an isolated ego, a disconnected mind, confronting a world of external things, free to make personal decisions with the goal of maximizing individual welfare.

It is to no avail to attack this utilitarian method by suggesting that it fails to account for non-economic motives such as the urge to charity. It is easy within the instrumentalist framework to extend the model to incorporate 'ethical' preferences so that a rational economic agent can trade-off a clear conscience against the convenience of using plastic bags or driving a gas guzzler.

The colonization by modern economics of all human behaviours and the social sciences that study them has been taken to its logical extreme by Chicago economist Gary Becker. It is a challenge to all economists to say where they diverge from Becker. Many would express disagreement, but most would also accept the view of 'environmental economics' that preservation of endangered species, filling the hole in the ozone layer and global deforestation are questions that are answered through rigorous application of cost-benefit analysis in which the relative importance of the destruction of the natural environment is to be measured by market or quasi-market prices.

The essential distortion of the modern economists' way of inventing the world lies not in the rationality or otherwise of consumer preferences but in the very construction of the individual and from there the relationship of the individual to the world. The human agent is reduced to a repository of instrumentalist desires which generate a series of actions. These actions—buying and selling goods—result in quanta of happiness which are deposited in the place occupied by the individual.

Hopelessly trapped in the world of things, economics imagines that the translation of the activities of the outside world into inwardly experienced human welfare—an intensely subtle and obscure process—is effected by one simple factor, the quantity of goods consumed.

NEUROTIC CONSUMPTION

The idea of consumer sovereignty—in which individual consumers are the only ones who know what is in their interests and that whatever they do is in their interests—is an exceedingly powerful one. Economists need never ask the uncomfortable question of what people really want from their consumer spending. It is irrelevant. It is not even worthy of comment. It is simply assumed that people want exactly what they buy—cars, clothes, books, holidays—and that they are fully conscious of their desires and needs. When social critics suggest that people are manipulated by advertising into buying things they do not want, or indeed things that are positively harmful to them, the critics are accused by the economists of elitism, of believing that they know better than ordinary people what is best for them. The sovereignty of the consumer is unchallengeable; the outcome of the marketplace receives moral blessing.

Yet we have known at least since Freud that our desires and needs are often unconscious and may lie beneath impenetrable layers of conscious and well-articulated beliefs about ourselves and our world. The most powerful of these conscious beliefs is that more wealth means more happiness, that growth is good.

For modern economics, if consumers are free to express their 'preferences' then they will maximize their welfare. One popular text states at the outset that the meaning of the term 'preference' is taken as understood. We all know what is meant by the statement 'I prefer this to that'. It is true that I can say that I prefer a jam doughnut to an orange. I can even say that I prefer an unspoiled wilderness to the income I might have from turning it into a pile of woodchips. But what does it mean for a person with an eating disorder to say 'I prefer a jam doughnut to an orange'? Perhaps the internal argument might run like this: 'I long for that jam doughnut, but if I eat it I will become fatter, I am unhappy when I am fat. Moreover (I know at a deeper level), I am not responding to any physical need but to my compulsive need for food, a need that arises from the absence of love and a loving self-image from my childhood. But I still prefer the jam doughnut.'

Despite awkward attempts to avoid it, the economist's argument that proceeds from the expression of individual preferences to human welfare always collapses into the tautology that whatever we choose, *ipso facto*, is best for us. For it can only be the calculating self-centered economic agent that is consistent with the political analogue of consumer sovereignty, the 'freedom' that is defended by liberal democracy. Consumer sovereignty is the foundation stone of the Western political system and that is why economists, the ideologists of that system, defend consumer sovereignty so vociferously.

Nevertheless, the economists' implicit supposition that the needs and desires that are being satisfied by consumer spending are no more than the needs and desires that they appear to satisfy—a jam doughnut satisfies the desire for a jam doughnut—is profoundly misleading if our goal really is to understand how to advance human well-being.

It is generally accepted that certain forms of consumption behavior are neurotic. I have already mentioned compulsive eating. A man who buys a red sports-car may feel a need to assert his sexual potency in order to compensate for a deeper feeling of inadequacy. Today, in a world of vast variety of choice among consumer goods, everything we buy becomes an expression of our personae, of our self-images projected onto the world. Once consumer spending began to exceed the level necessary to ensure that our basic needs were met, the possibility of neurotic consumption became not only real but nigh unavoidable. Consumption became a means of attempting to satisfy our deeper psychological needs, a weakness quick to be understood and exploited by advertisers. Now our entire culture of consumption is neurotic. Our obsession with the acquisition of material goods and money (the power over goods) is above all else a compulsive and futile attempt to overcome the pervasive and entrenched feeling of emptiness in our lives, however that feeling of emptiness may manifest itself in the character of each person.

I will argue that consumer spending serves in our society as a hollow attempt to achieve what we *truly* desire as beings, transcendence. If I am right then modern economics is wholly preoccupied with the analysis of futile human behaviour.

ATMAN AND THE ATMAN PROJECT

We have come to accept that what people want, what each of us wants, is just the good life, to be left untroubled by doubts as we pursue material comfort, status, family harmony and friendships. We have an enormous investment in convincing ourselves that these are what we want because they are all that life appears to offer. To compare, as I am, this prosaic world with some deep yearning for the meaning of life seems pompous, intellectual and perhaps a little obsessive. But this latter perception is itself a product of the trivialisation of our inner lives, of our true purpose, of the deeper urges that we sublimate unmercifully. In our age, to ask questions about the meaning of life has become a joke; the joke tells us that there is no meaning.

Yet at some level each of knows what we really want. The fundamental desire has not changed over the millennia of human history. It is based on an inescapable awareness of the cosmic vastness in which we live out our 70 years on this planet. We know that inside there is a watcher—faceless, transparent, without attribute, an awareness that has no boundaries, a consciousness that, because of its very nature, is identical in all of us. Humans have been both blessed and cursed with this awareness. We are distinguished from other forms of life by the fact that the gift of consciousness allows us, indeed, compels us to contemplate the sense of our existence. Thus Ernest Becker can adumbrate the wisdom of the sages: ' . . . what man really fears is not so much extinction, but extinction with *insignificance*'.[4] Surely there is nothing so insignificant in this vast timeless cosmos than the little ego self, the character we identify with and present to the world. But when extinction of the true Self is no more than a merging with the Absolute, there can be no fear.

If our goal and purpose is realization of the true Self, what cruel substitutes the utility functions of the economists are. They feed our little ego selves but can provide no nourishment for the true Self. Our lone real desire is transcendence—total identification with the universal watcher within, unity with the godhead. When we contrast our true desire to achieve transcendence with the false promise of economics, much of the conflict and turmoil within our selves and in our societies begins to be understood. This is the essence of the brilliant thesis of Ken Wilber which is summarized in the following passage from his book, *Up From Eden:*

> Because man wants real transcendence above all else, but because he will not accept the necessary death of his separate-self sense, he goes about seeking transcendence in ways that *actually prevent* it and force symbolic substitutes. And these substitutes come in all varieties: sex, food, money, fame, knowledge, power—all are ultimately substitute gratifications, simple substitutes for true release in Wholeness. This is why human desire is insatiable, why all joys yearn for infinity—all a person wants is Atman; all he finds are substitutes for it.[5]

We really seek Atman—transcendence, unity consciousness, merger with the godhead—but we have temporarily forgotten this fact. While we feel the sense of yearning with all of its existential force, it seems that all we can do is substitute other goals for the attainment of Atman; these become our Atman projects.

The implications for modern economics and the societies it dominates are profound indeed. We begin to get an inkling of why we appear to be driven by unquenchable desire, why it is that we *never* have enough money or enough status or enough power. The urge to accumulate is irresistible and incessant; it is incessant because the things that we want, the things we accumulate, are not the things that can satisfy our true needs. We want roses to grow in our gardens but we continue to plant weeds; yet our desire for roses is insatiable. We play on ourselves a monumental trick. Why?

If we want roses why do we not cultivate roses? If our true goal is transcendence—individuation, wholeness, the godhead—and this is the only goal that can truly give meaning to our lives—the agonizing but unconscious need to understand why we sit on this tiny isolated planet with a huge capacity for consciousness of our earthly state and our relationship with the Universe—if this is our true goal, why do we not forsake all else and aim precisely at that? The reason is simple: to attain that true goal, that state of transcendence, requires that we pass through death, the death of the ego, of the worldly self. Fear of annihilation is the ultimate terror. We fear death of the ego because, so closely do we identify with our egos, we believe that ego-death means total annihilation. In fear of annihilation we engage in endless endeavours to prove our significance, to stamp ourselves on the little worlds or the big worlds that surround us.

The dominant mode of striving for this immortality in Western industrial society is the accumulation of wealth. Making money is an immortality project. We invest our selves in material goods and money; instead of becoming our possessions, they own us. Rich men build empires and have their names put on buildings and on sporting grounds. The bigger these monuments the better. Some build monuments to themselves, some leave dynasties and some leave only gravestones. However we do it, we hope that we will have changed the world and left our mark; annihilation will not be total.

Our lives then revolve around a delusion. All we really want is enlightenment, the realization of why we are here and thus merger with the Absolute. Yet we do not understand this consciously; we only experience the yearning that this need gives to our daily lives. To satisfy this yearning we substitute the accumulation of money, the amassing of power, the proving of our sexual vitality and the piling up of fame.

These substitute gratifications are cruel, for they both fail to appease our appetites and whet our appetites for more.

Who is it that craves these gratifications? It is the isolated ego, the trickster within. Our sense of being a separate individual, the isolated ego inside our bodies, is nothing but a *substitute* for the true Self, a concentration of universal consciousness. It seems to us that our separate self is the centre of the cosmos and the gratification of its worldly needs is the purpose of life; the substitute subject in pursuit of the substitute object. It is the death of the substitute subject that we fear most of all. Yet it is only the death of the isolated ego that can give us what we truly want. This is the great irony of human life and the secret of all spiritual traditions.[6]

The world of modern economics is constructed entirely within the realm of substitute objects and *homo economicus* is no more or less than the substitute subject. Economics has developed the great illusion to its most refined expression. It takes the substitute self, the ego self, as the starting point of human activity, and builds a theory about how substitute objects—consumer goods—fulfil the desires of the substitute subject. As such, economics provides the most sophisticated justification for and elaboration of the great illusion. This separation of subject and object, the splitting of the divine unity, is the root cause of human misery.

ECOLOGY AND ETHICS

In recent years, the environment movement has provided a most serious challenge to the political and personal hegemony of economics. At its deeper levels, environmentalism is a reassertion of the divine unity. Although its objections to economics are mostly ill-formed, there is an immovable opinion that economics cannot provide the solutions to the Earth's environmental problems. At the heart of the environmentalists' objection to economics is the refusal by environmentalists to abandon the belief that ethical principles matter.

The economic way of thinking begins and ends with utility, the 'satisfaction' people get from consuming goods. People are thought deliberately to calculate the benefits of one set of consumption choices, compare them with the benefits of others and decide which one will make them most happy. This applies to buying a car or to deciding complex environmental questions such as whether to log a thousand-year-old forest or to drain a mangrove swamp. For neoclassical economics, if the net utility of the gainers from an activity outweighs the net disutility of the losers, then society benefits from the activity and it should go ahead—in the economist's lexicon it is a 'potential Pareto improvement'.

The process of comparing costs and benefits to maximize net satisfaction *determines* whether an action is right or wrong. This is the nineteenth-century philosophy of utilitarianism, one that has been uniformly rejected by social sciences other than economics. Economists generally do not recognize utilitarianism as one of several possible moral philosophies but believe that it just describes how the world is.

We have argued that the utilitarian approach renders redundant the ethical aspects of decisions. It excludes morality because the calculus of utility itself determines what is right and wrong. An action is right if the increase in utility of the gainers outweighs the decline in utility of the losers. It would make no sense for the economist to argue that one of the benefits of taking a particular decision—such as damming a river, declaring a national park or saving a species from extinction—is the 'utility' to be had from 'doing the right thing'. To determine what is the right thing is the purpose of the economic calculus.

The 1970s and 1980s saw an enormous increase in the influence of free market ideas, beginning with monetarism and broadening into the full-blown economic rationalism of the late 1980s. This involved a sustained attack on the role of government and the validity of community decision making. The great increase in interdependence among national economies through the liberalization of trade and financial markets has meant that international economic forces hold national economies in their sway. Governments, in the pursuit of growth at all costs, have abandoned control over the economic lives of their citizens; if international financiers decide that inflation is more important than unemployment then millions more must join the dole queues. All decisions are being turned over to private markets and by that act the social and ethical aspects of economic decisions are cast out. Only money flows matter for they alone express values. If the private financial benefits of a development outweigh the private financial costs then, the economic rationalists tell us, the development is a good thing. It matters not that a community may suffer when it is dispossessed of its source of aesthetic or spiritual nourishment. If the community cannot raise the funds to buy what it already owns then its 'preferences' are redundant.

Environmental issues are fundamentally ethical issues to which economic calculation must be made subordinate. We have a right to clean air and pure water; sacred places speak to us more powerfully than any sum of money, if only we could listen; it is wrong that creatures that are being driven to extinction in the pursuit of profit should go 'unrepresented' because their supporters are not rich enough to save them. To pretend that environmental questions can be resolved by economic calculation robs us of our ethical natures, the very quality that makes us human. When we forget our ethical selves we deny our unity with the natural world, the world that sustains life. *Homo economicus* is suicidal—'killing ourselves slowly and by degrees, dismembering our own Natures'; only humanity aware of its divinity can survive.

The deep attachment of Western societies to economic growth becomes explicable when we recognize that the hidden urge that growth seeks to satisfy cannot be satisfied by growth. The psychological roots of our obsession with growth go directly to the struggle between our worldly selves and our divine natures. As long as we deny our divinity, deny our unity with the whole and suppress our primordial desire to achieve transcendence, then we will be endlessly preoccupied with material enrichment through economic growth, and in consequence we will remain doomed to spiritual impoverishment.

The basic position of many in the environmental movement is that continued growth is inconsistent with long-term material well-being and with social equity. Many in the environmental movement would also agree that continuing growth is inconsistent with our true goal, transcendence. Even in the absence of the current and impending ecological disasters that will constrain economic growth, growth can never bring contentment and purpose to our lives. The ecological crisis now confronting the globe only serves to reinforce the self-defeating nature of the materialist Atman project.

What I am proposing is not so much an appeal to higher moral principles but an appeal for the most profound psychological transformation, a transformation that would not only result in casting off the immorality of rapaciousness but also a return to an essentially religious view of self, life and the world.

The essential morality that flows from this is not something that is brought about by persuasion but one that emerges naturally from a state of harmony with the world. It is a plea to allow oneself to cast off the immiserising strictures of the ego—with all of its pride, materialism, desire, rivalry and obsessive rationality—and to embrace a world beyond the shallow, exterior world of things that serves as a veil obscuring our true selves.

IN CONCLUSION

To the economist, the world is described by the archetypal economic situation in which the consumer, an isolated, distinct individual defined by a set of preferences and in possession of an income, confronts an array of goods with the aim of maximizing his or her welfare.

In this scheme, we as humans and the world as a system are driven by our ego selves, the little selves that are defined by their separateness, by their confrontation with the natural world, by their self-centeredness and by their competition with each other. The little self swims in the sea of the mind; it is subject to the sway of ideas; its knowledge is constrained by rationality.

While this eternal truth is expressed most explicitly in the Eastern religious traditions it is also the essential knowledge that Christ imparted. In the view of this non-Christian, a Christian is one who knows the big Self—the Self that transcends the boundaries of the body, the Self that can merge with the cosmos, the Self that knows that the Kingdom of God can only be within us. The big Self knows the nature of the world and our role in it not through logic and belief but through immediate appreciation, divine revelation, of what is and what we are.

As long as we live in the world of modern economics—the world of material things, of competition, of exclusive rationality, of conflict with the natural environment, which is to say, the world of separateness—we cannot be close to god because it is precisely that veil of separateness, that cloud of unknowing, that exists to provide us with the challenge to find god and thereby to give sense to our existence.

In the archetypal situation of the economist it is not only the separateness of the consumer that from the outset denies god to us, it is the pursuit of pleasure as well. The theory and the practice in which the objective of human activity is to maximize the personal returns from allocating our income poisons our relationship with god because the divine is driven from our hearts.

Jesus said that it is easier for a camel to pass through the eye of a needle than for a rich man to enter the Kingdom of Heaven. The rich man is in this respect no different from the man who wants to be rich, who strives for riches. But what is the Kingdom of Heaven? It is where god dwells. And where is the Kingdom of Heaven? Christ tells us: the Kingdom of Heaven is within us. This is the mystical truth of all religious experience—of the Native American, of the Hindu sage, of the Christian mystic, of the Bodhisattva, of the Australian Aborigine dreaming. In the words of Kashmir Shaivism; 'God dwells *within* you, as you'.

Jesus' admonition about the fate of the rich man does not mean that some supernatural being adjudicates from on high declaring "Ah, that man is greedy, he shall not enter my kingdom". In saying that god dwells within us Jesus meant something very literal—that god's home is within our hearts. 'Blessed are the pure in heart, for they shall see God.' So that as we fill our hearts with desire for riches or fame or worldly success we drive out god. 'You cannot serve God and mammon.'

And when we take the archetypal economic situation of the isolated consumer choosing between various goods in order to maximize personal pleasure we are, in Biblical parlance, committing sins, three sins, acts that take us as humans away from god.

We commit the sin of separation, of imagining ourselves to be no more than isolated egos inside our bodies each with an individual free will.

We commit the sin of calculation whereby in the act of calculating how our welfare can be maximized we are guilty of selfishness and the affirmation of our self-separateness.

We commit the sin of mammon, the belief that the path to happiness is through acquisition of those things that can be had for money.

A Christian is one who has taken the god of Jesus Christ into her or his heart. If one has truly done this then modern economics can have no credibility. Indeed, so far as one believes that we as humans are accurately portrayed by economics, then the teachings of Christ can have no place except as rootless moralizing.

Perhaps it might be thought that I am guilty of generalizing, that we can divide our lives into a secular part in which modern economics describes our behavior and a spiritual part in which we can admit god. Personally, I cannot understand how this can be true. For admitting god into oneself actually *defines* oneself as a being, a being utterly remote from that described by *homo economicus*. Indeed, it is more accurate to say that the individual of economics is what we are destined to struggle against and transcend—to transcend our sense of separation, to transcend the desires and the cunning of our egos, to transcend the lure of a society devoted to material pleasures.

Look at that society. What does it tell us loud and insistent? How pivotal is consumption to everything. How ubiquitous and penetrating is consumer advertising. How unrelenting is the assertion of our individuality. How unthinkable it is to imagine a society without economic growth. One cannot walk a path between these beliefs and divinity, except as an anguished wandering of indecision.

1 Morris Berman, *The Reenchantment of the World* (Cornell University Press, Ithaca 1981) p. 16

2 Berman, *ibid.*, p. 16

3 See, for instance, Joseph Campbell, *Myths To Live By* (Bantam Books, New York, 1973).

4 Ernest Becker, *Escape From Evil* (The Free Press, New York 1975) p. 4

5 Ken Wilber, *Up From Eden: A Transpersonal View of Human Evolution* (Shambhala, Boston 1986) p. 13

6 'To avoid the instantaneous death of transcendence, people kill themselves slowly and by degrees, dismembering their own Natures in order to preserve their own selves.' (Ken Wilber, *op. cit.*, p. 77)

INDEX